PRAISE FOR *THE PASSION CONVERSATION*

"It's a fast read, a fun read, a smart read. Short sentences, huge heart. Read it. Why? To absorb an important truth from the masters of word of mouth movements: Conversations spring from passions, not products."

>—Dan Heath, co-author of *Decisive, Switch,* and *Made to Stick*

"Have you ever gotten teary-eyed over a business book? Better yet, over your own business? Prepare yourself for *The Passion Conversation*, where the folks at Brains on Fire tell how their business connected them with people in very moving and powerful ways, redefining words like marketing, sales, and success. Read this book to move your perspective from business to people, and experience the incredible effect it will have on your life and work."

>—Jon Mueller, General Manager of 800-CEO-READ

"Love is the missing ingredient in developing loyalty with customers. In *The Passion Conversation,* the smart folks at Brains on Fire expertly explain how to develop deeper connections with customers who in turn sing your praises to everyone they know."

>—Jackie Huba, author of *Monster Loyalty: How Lady Gaga Turns Followers into Fanatics*

"I've had my eye on Brains on Fire for a while. Their humanity makes them quite distinctive, and *The Passion Conversation* captures that unique voice."

>—Peter Sims, author of *Little Bets*, and founder of The BLK SHP Enterprises

Brains on Fire

Join the conversation at brainsonfire.com/blog.

Understanding, Sparking, and Sustaining
Word of Mouth Marketing

THE PASSION CONVERSATION

ROBBIN PHILLIPS | GREG CORDELL | GENO CHURCH | AND JOHN MOORE

WILEY

Cover image: Nathan Spainhour
Cover design: Eric B. Whitlock and Rachel G. Bass

Published by John Wiley & Sons, Inc., Hoboken, New Jersey.
Published simultaneously in Canada.

NPS®, Net Promoter® & Net Promoter® Score are registered trademarks of Satmetrix Systems, Inc., Bain & Company, and Fred Reichheld.

Limit of Liability/Disclaimer of Warranty: While the publisher and author have used their best efforts in preparing this book, they make no representations or warranties with the respect to the accuracy or completeness of the contents of this book and specifically disclaim any implied warranties of merchantability or fitness for a particular purpose. No warranty may be created or extended by sales representatives or written sales materials. The advice and strategies contained herein may not be suitable for your situation. You should consult with a professional where appropriate. Neither the publisher nor the author shall be liable for damages arising herefrom.

For general information about our other products and services, please contact our Customer Care Department within the United States at (800) 762-2974, outside the United States at (317) 572-3993 or fax (317) 572-4002.

Wiley publishes in a variety of print and electronic formats and by print-on-demand. Some material included with standard print versions of this book may not be included in e-books or in print-on-demand. If this book refers to media such as a CD or DVD that is not included in the version you purchased, you may download this material at http://booksupport.wiley.com. For more information about Wiley products, visit www.wiley.com.

Library of Congress Cataloging-in-Publication Data:

Phillips, Robbin.
    The passion conversation : understanding, sparking, and sustaining word of mouth marketing / Robbin Phillips, Greg Cordell, Geno Church and John Moore.
      pages cm
      Includes index.
      ISBN 978-1-118-53333-8 (cloth); ISBN 978-1-118-76794-8 (ebk);
      ISBN 978-1-118-76830-3 (ebk)
      1. Word-of-mouth advertising.   2. Business referrals.   3. Marketing.   I. Title.
    HF5827.95.P45   2013
    658.8'72—dc23
                                                                        20130194
Printed in the United States of America.
10 9 8 7 6 5 4 3 2 1

This book is dedicated to the heroes, the driven, the wonderers, the rebels, to those who answer a calling—to those who wear their hearts on their sleeves and 146 on their hearts. You remind us that becoming more human is the journey to greatness for any brand. Because ultimately, the best brands, the brands we love most, are the ones that never let us forget how it feels to be good people.

Contents

Preface   A Note from the Authors   ix

Introduction   1

Chapter One   Understanding Word of Mouth Marketing   17

Chapter Two   Sparking Word of Mouth Marketing   37

Chapter Three   Heroes: A Love Story   69

Chapter Four   The Fitness Rebellion: A Love Story   97

Chapter Five   The Driven Class: A Love Story   123

Chapter Six   Wonderopolis: A Love Story   149

Chapter Seven   Sustaining Word of Mouth Marketing   177

Bibliography   196

Acknowledgments   198

About the Authors   201

Index   205

Preface

A Note from the Authors:

We won't lie. This was a hard book to write.

You see, at Brains on Fire, we believe that we owe it to our courageous customers to spend most of our time and efforts finding and sharing their passion conversation and growing their tribes. As people who *practice* word of mouth marketing, just finding time to write this book was a really, really big deal.

We burned some serious late-night oil.

But it was worth it because we learned so much along the way. And we grew even closer to our customers. We had someone ask us the other day, "Aren't you afraid you're giving away your secrets?" We smiled and said, "Nope." See, we don't believe there are any marketing secrets. We've learned that sharing and connecting with other like-minded people in the world is what's magical these days. By sharing knowledge with others, we've learned *good things will happen.*

Our first book, *Brains on Fire: Igniting Powerful, Sustainable, Word of Mouth Movements* (yes, Brains on Fire is the name of our company *and* our first book) was a really remarkable ride. It connected us with some super-cool people. Some of those people have become our friends and kindred spirits. Some of them knocked on our door and joined our tribe. Some we're honored to call our customers and advocates. You'll get to meet a lot of them in the following pages.

Consider this book a continuation of the lessons we shared in our first book. Here's a quick review:

Movements aren't about the product conversation; they're about the *passion* conversation.

They start with the first conversation.

They have inspirational leadership.

They have a barrier of entry.

They empower people with knowledge.

They create a feeling of shared ownership.

They have powerful identities.

They live both online and offline.

They make advocates feel like rock stars.

Many times they find and fight an injustice.

And most importantly, movements get results.

We love hearing people recite these lessons back to us. We love it when they let us know how they have applied some of them to their own businesses. And you'll absolutely see the lessons from our last book brought to life throughout these pages. Still, we knew we had learned more in the three years since our first book was published, and we wanted to spend some time digging deeper. We felt that we owed it to our readers, our customers, and ourselves.

We're big believers in the notion that writing (*and speaking*) inspires thinking, and writing this book and telling these stories has truly been a gift to us. We've talked to many wise and wonderful people including our customers, their customers, and even each other. Writing this book and having these conversations has helped us really *think* about the work we're doing in the world and define what matters. It has helped us grow. It has opened our hearts, and helped us fall even deeper in love with the people we serve.

Our only hope is that it does a little bit of the same for you.

With LOVE always,
Robbin, Greg, Geno, and John
(and the entire Brains on Fire tribe)

A LITTLE SIDENOTE FROM THE AUTHORS

When you have a book with four authors, you have to make some style decisions. So just like several other author teams have opted to do, we talk about ourselves in the third person. Please know that none us ever, ever, ever refers to ourselves in the third person when you're actually with us face-to-face. (Geez, that's weird when people do that.) We did it here to make it easier to follow. You'll even see us quote ourselves. Think of it this way: We simply decided to let you inside our walls and let you listen in on our passion conversations: conversations with our clients, our teammates, some smart people we know, and even among ourselves. Enjoy. And do us a favor: Please reach out to us and let us know what you think. You can find us thinking out loud most days on our blog at www.brainsonfire.com.

The Passion Conversation is a LOVE STORY.

We know what you're probably thinking: The last thing the world needs is another business book.

Don't worry. This is *not* a business book. This is a love story.

It might sound strange, but hear us out. *The Passion Conversation* is a story about being famous for the people who love you, *for the way you love them.*

We're going to share some remarkable *love* stories.

In the three years since our first book, *Brains on Fire*, was published we've done a lot of thinking about *love* and how it relates to business and to word of mouth marketing. We've also given a lot of thought to the word *passion*, which we actually mention 67 times in our last book. (Sixty-seven times? Yup. John Moore, the self proclaimed "ticky-tacky detail geek" among us counted.)

Since that first book, we've wondered over and over again—at first to ourselves, then aloud to one another—is passion something that can be unearthed in someone? Can it be taught? Is it real? It is overused or misused? Did *we* misuse it one or more of those 67 times? Does it belong in business, or is it a word best saved for artists, romance novels, religious stories, or 20-year-old lovebirds who can't stand the thought of being apart?

We've asked ourselves over the years why the following lesson from our last book gets tweeted and repeated over and over and over again.

> ## "It's not about the product conversation; it's about the passion conversation."

Hmmmm.

The book you're holding in your hands is called *The Passion Conversation.* We don't take that deliberate choice of words lightly. Can we really write a book worthy of such a lofty title? Who knows? But we do know the following:

We're all in marketing grad school. And there are some valuable *lessons* to be learned inside the passionate love stories we're about to share with you. They're lessons that can make our businesses better places to work. Lessons that can make us feel more alive and more purposeful in how we spend our time and talents. Lessons that can help spark social change. Think about it: Can you imagine a world where more of us are happy at work? A world where the majority of us are working with passion?

In the following pages, we'll share the stories of four amazing organizations—Foundations Recovery Network, Anytime Fitness, DeVry University, and the National Center for Family Literacy—that took the time and effort to bring their passion conversations to life inside and outside of their office walls. Regardless of their for-profit or not-for-profit status, each of the companies we're highlighting is adding value to people's lives, and in doing so, they're sparking word of mouth.

It's in our DNA as human beings to share things we find valuable and meaningful with others. We talk about things *(and people)* we love often and with a force that sticks. You might not be a recovery business, a fitness franchise, a higher education university, a not-for-profit, or any of the other businesses we've sprinkled in, but chances are these stories will inspire you to take action nonetheless.

We believe with all our hearts and souls, it is possible, absolutely possible, to fall madly and passionately in love with the people you serve.

And we believe that it's possible for those folks to fall in love with *you*, too; and, yes, for you to become famous and grow your organization because of that love. If you want people to be in love with you and talk about you, you must fall in love with them *first.* Your clients, customers, donors, tribe, employees, advocates— what you call them doesn't really matter—can and should become beloved heroes in your organizations.

Because guess what naturally happens when you're in love? You talk about that person you love constantly. You can't wait to be with them. You think about how you can surprise them. You inspire them. They inspire you. You share secrets. You want to understand them. You have empathy. You defend them. You have compassion. You don't mind taking out the trash. You are deeply connected.

Passion is contagious.

As business owners, marketers, or Chief Love Officers (*a title we think more relevant than Chief Marketing Officer*) we should feel wildly romantic and passionate about the people who help fuel our businesses and spread our causes. Passion fuels word of mouth conversation and excitement. Our passions make us happy and let us know that life is worth living. They motivate us to do remarkable things. When we are passionate about someone, we really do talk about that person all the time. We're eager and excited to share the tiniest details. Spend just a few minutes around a new parent and you'll see what we mean.

Passion is not something you *own*; it's something you pass forward. So if you take the time to understand your own unique passion conversations—*and yes, we believe everyone has them*—as well as the ones that excite those you serve, something amazing will happen.

That's exactly what we've done to grow our own business over the years. Not only have we fallen in love with our customers, we received the permission and indeed the honor to get to know and care for our customers' customers. We are village matchmakers, facilitators, the Cupid of marketing companies. It's our role to help connect our customers with their employees and customers through *shared passions*.

Don't just take our word for it.

We've studied the work of some smart people who are also digging deep into *why* people talk—we've even become friends with a few. We've mixed and kneaded some of our in-the-trenches knowledge with the areas they've been researching and learning. We found that there's magic in that recipe, magic we feel compelled to share with the world.

What does it take to fall in love with your advocates, the customers and employees who are ready, willing, and happy to fall in love with you? The people who therefore willingly and passionately talk about you?

Here are the key things we've learned that you'll see come alive in the following pages:

1. **Know yourself and clearly define what you really want from a relationship with your employees and customers.** We hate it when we hear companies talk about *using* fans to tell their story. Think about it: Do

you really *use* people you care about? Absolutely *not*. You *listen* to them. You *get close* to them. You see them frequently. You want to be a meaningful part of their life. When we begin working with a new client, we almost always start by listening to stories within that organization's walls. We have a day of knowledge sharing. We play games. We laugh. We hear their hopes and dreams. Our goal is to help the people we serve better define who they are and what they stand for. So, we spend time with the people who answer the phones. We observe them in action as they talk with their current and potential customers and supporters. We ask to see their love letters. We take photos of the things they hang on their walls and keep at their desks. We talk to the people on the front lines as well as the CMOs and CEOs and brand managers. We spend time in meetings and just hang out socially to get know their passions. Because you know what? *Passion should be a mirror.* Write that down or star it in the margins so you get it under your fingernails. The reflections should match; inside passion should mirror outside passion. You have to know what drives you and your employees to get up in the morning before you can connect with other like-minded people. As author and speaker Simon Sinek says in his book *Start with Why,* we go looking for your *why. (By the way, if you haven't read Simon's book, do it. Right after you're done with this one.)*

2. **Be very realistic about who your customers and potential customers really are.** If you're a not-for-profit, get an accurate picture of your volunteers and your donors. Who's doing more than just writing a check once or twice a year and *why*? Start internally and ask yourself some tough questions. Who do you serve?

What do they really look like? What are their challenges? How and when do you fit in their lives? How can you add value?

For a brief time, we had a client in the beauty and fashion business. We discovered this client's customers were fairly average women, people who shopped at Walmart and Target and drove minivans. They were amazing, beautiful women who cared about looking their best, but they were not just off the cover of *Vogue* or *Glamour*. So we connected with them and started igniting a community around that connection. We found that they were real women with beauty and fashion tips and life stories (and struggles) to share. The CEO was upset that the women we felt they should be celebrating *and loving* weren't magazine-glossy perfect. Some of them *(heaven forbid!)* were even overweight. He wanted to chase the pretty girl at the party, because that's who he wanted leading the community and talking on his company's behalf. That's what people in the beauty industry do. But the pretty girl in the room didn't want to talk to him and his brand. He missed the point entirely, and we resigned. Most likely, before we were about to be fired.

The point is you have to be very realistic about who your customers really are and not just who you want them to be. As most of us know from personal experiences, you can't make someone who is not interested in you love you. Write this down too: You can't choose your advocates; *they choose you.*

3. **You can't find love sitting on your couch watching TV.** There's a time to just chill and watch TV, just like there is a time to quietly pore over data and

demographics. Make no mistake: We love data as much as the next company, but to really fall in love with your customers and find their passions, you have take time to *be* with your customers. You have to get out and make real world connections. You have to meet people where they are. Join their parties and go to their football games. And for goodness sake, don't just come out and ask people, "What is your passion?" It's a personal and emotional question and one that's pretty hard to answer without any warning or opportunity for forethought. You have to earn trust to learn about someone's true passions and trust takes time. Let's be honest. The first requirement in finding the passion conversation is pretty simple: *You have to enjoy being with people.*

4. **You can discover love and learn a lot online.** There are tons of ways to listen to and participate in the conversations your customers and potential customers are having online. We partner with many smart companies who can help do just that. So exactly what *can* you learn from listening to these online conversations? A lot. You might find out people are tuning you out, or that they are crying *bullshit* on your entire industry. By using today's online technology, everyone has the ability to meet people who share similar interests, people who they would have never been able to meet in "real life."

When we get a new client, we do two Google searches: "I love _____(fill in client name)." And "I hate _____(fill in client name)." This helps us narrow down where the passionate conversations, both positive and negative, are taking place. You can learn a lot about passion at both ends of the emotional spectrum.

5. **Love is patient and kind.** You cannot find the passion conversation, ignite community and fall in love overnight. Sure, there are one-night stands that might feel good at the time *(perhaps the marketing equivalent of this is a successful campaign)*. But for real and lasting relationships to take hold, you have to be in it for the long haul. As we stated in our last book, igniting community and sparking movements are not like traditional ad campaigns. Ad campaigns have an on and off switch. You create them, run them, cross your fingers and hope for the best. Building community and loving your customers is not something you do for a limited amount of time. It's something you do every single day. And the value of that effort grows exponentially stronger and deeper with time.

6. **Meeting people through activities is a low-pressure way of getting to know them, and also will encourage bonding.** We almost always bring our customers together with their potential community leaders, something we discussed at length in *Brains on Fire*'s Lesson #3, which focused on the fact that movements have inspirational leadership. We bring them together to engage in a multiday summit or training session in an impressive venue. We encourage everyone to let go and enjoy themselves as we learn about each other. People share and form trust, and memories are created.

There's a little secret in the dating world that *The Game* author Neil Strauss calls "time-distortion." (Though definitely not a business book, there are few good marketing lessons hidden in there.) "Time-distortion" occurs when you go to several different places with a person or group you've just met in a short period of

Called to Serve WITH _____.

    Before you can take your passion conversation outside of your organization, you have to make sure it's felt deeply and clearly inside its own walls.

    Bon Secours St. Francis Health System is one of our current customers. They've actually been a lifelong customer of Robbin's. Seriously, she's worked with them through her entire entrepreneurial career. Together we've seen them through three CEOs and numerous CMOs. We were even with them when they changed leadership hands to an entirely new Catholic Health System based out of Maryland.

    During their first CEO's tenure, St. Francis employees truly let their faith shine. They prayed before meetings and surgeries and nuns were often seen walking the halls and visiting patients in their rooms. The staff openly and proudly shared what made St. Francis different as a health provider.

    The second CEO felt it was better to rein that difference in a bit and instead focus on the technology aspect of health care. Given the research available at the time this was seemingly not a bad move. Unfortunately, not long after this change, turnover and low morale became an issue. Something was clearly missing...

    When the third and current CEO, Mark Nantz, came on board he and his team made a bold decision to return St. Francis to its core values and reason for being. Together with the HR and marketing departments, we began working on a plan to discover the motivation of every single person in the organization. Everyone. The first step was to take a day and meet offsite with the entire 200+ person leadership team. We asked each person why they were in patient care, and more specifically why they were a part of the Bon Secours St. Francis team. These individuals were then given the tools to ask others throughout the organization those same questions.

    For the next few months these leaders and trainers held offsite retreats with different groups and departments to help each individual determine their own personal response to the prompt "Called to serve with _____." Their answer revealed the passion and emotions behind their work. Were they called to serve with love, joy, patience, simplicity, humor, the healing ministry of Christ? The answer didn't matter; the goal was to simply connect their personal passion with the higher mission of the health system.

We produced a video for the training sessions showcasing simple photos of people at work along with the following narration:

We can do more with than we can ever do without.

With talent and expertise, with bold ideas and compassion, ever aware of the impact our actions have on others, even when the action is simply to be ... with.

So, with is how we stand. As Christ stood with those left to stand alone.

His Touch we share. His Healing we minister.

That we might lift hearts and connect every life we are called to serve ... with love.

In addition to the offsite training, Daily Huddles were initiated throughout the organization. These five- to ten-minute sharing sessions allow and encourage team members to relate their own personal "with _____ " moments.

So what's changed in the two years since this internal movement was sparked? According to Mark, employee turnover rates are down from double digits to single digits, a remarkable change in such a short time. Also employee and physician Gallup satisfaction scores are at an all-time high. And more importantly patient care scores have improved.

Just recently we re-edited the original "Called to Serve with _____ " video and turned it into a 60-second television spot. The community's response has been absolutely overwhelming. Love letters have poured in. The employees now stand proud when their friends and family share their connection to and love of their mission.

There are so many lessons in this story but one stands out far and above: People work better, and in this case provide better care, when they are more engaged and it's easier to be engaged when your passions are allowed to shine.

time. Maybe you first go bowling, then to a restaurant, then out for ice cream, then for a nightcap. By creating memories in several different locations, it seems like you've known each other for longer than just one evening. This approach makes sense; after all, we feel more familiar around people with whom we've shared fun places and experiences. And while this takes time and effort in business relationships, it's worth it.

7. **Be realistic and take a stand.** You'll make some mistakes along the way and you'll even change your mind. You'll encounter a few dead ends while building lasting relationships and igniting community with your customers and your employees. This can get frustrating, but don't give up. *Keep going.* It's important to enjoy the process of expanding your community and connecting through shared passions. Not everyone will love you when you take a strong stand, and that's okay. You won't be everyone's cup of tea, so don't take it personally. You don't have to— in fact it's impossible to connect with everyone. You might even push a few people away, but that will actually turn out for the best since the people who are turned off by your passions will never be your advocates or customers.

8. **Become familiar.** Studies have shown that proximity is a significant factor in falling in love. The more someone becomes familiar to you, the more positive emotions you will feel around them—and the more the attraction increases. In order to get closer to someone, you need to have lots of contact with them. How can you provide platforms and content that add frequent, maybe even *daily* value? How can you create events that bond you to your clients? How can you give more than you get?

Once a year at Brains on Fire we bring in our employees and current and potential customers together for the Fire Sessions, a day of sharing and learning. We invite speakers we've met in our travels to share their research, experiences, and stories. We eat together, we talk, we laugh, and most importantly, we share. People start connecting with us months in advance, asking when the Fire Sessions are going to be, and if they can bring a friend. It's a lot of work, but it's one of our favorite events because *everyone* in our company gets to interact with our customers and advocates. And good things happen. For starters, we remember our *why*—something that does wonders to refuel our passion conversations.

9. **Tell some secrets.** A few of you reading this book know what a struggle it's been for us to find time to write it because we've let you in on that secret. More than once, we have tossed up our hands and said, "The world doesn't need another business book." Seriously. If you've shelled out the money to buy this book, you're in the club and we're planning on sharing the truth with you about the word of mouth marketing work we do. We're going to let you listen in on the *actual conversations* we have had with our customers, and *their* customers. There are a whole lot of quotes in this book. You'll hear many voices, including those from academics. We actually called people up, pressed the record button, and had those conversations transcribed. We even interviewed each other. That's how we wrote this book. There should be many, many authors of this book, but our publishers would only let us list four. We have notebooks full of those transcribed conversations. *(If you're ever in our neck of the woods, stop by and you can pore through all those words and dig even deeper.)*

We're going to share the good and the bad here because we all know what distinguishes a close friend or a romantic partner from any other random acquaintances: *the things you share with them.* Sharing shows you care, which leads to trust. So think about some ways you can you let your employees and customers in on things that they don't typically get to see. Doing so will create intimacy and closeness. It's contrary to normal business practices, but give it a try. The "first to know, first to tell" knowledge has been a longtime tenet of word of mouth marketing, and there's another benefit of sharing secrets: Your customers will get more comfortable in sharing *their* secrets *and trusting* you. Like all good relationships, it's a matter of give and take.

10. **Less is more.** The world is drowning in literature full of facts and figures that just don't stick. Don't create brochures; create *conversation tools.* And keep in mind that less is more when it comes to these. Think about something as simple as a lowly T-shirt. Consider how a T-shirt with "Break the Stigma" written on it invites a conversation. A hand-painted, one-of-a-kind Fitness Rebel T-shirt with your name on it invites a conversation. Less is more when it comes to stories as well. Short, sharable stories rule.

11. **The passion conversation isn't about getting people to talk about YOU, the brand. It's about getting people to talk about themselves.** Encourage others to talk about themselves, their lives, their hopes, and their dreams. Create platforms, online and offline, for the people you serve to share their own stories. Give them opportunities to talk and be willing to listen.

It's possible *to learn* to fall madly in love with your employees and your customers, and in the process unearth your own passion conversation. And this book is going to help you do just that.

We're not really in the marketing business these days. We're in the people business.

This makes sense for us because marketing nowadays is more about reframing the work you do in the world to inspire your employees and customers. The most successful word of mouth–driven businesses in the world have always been in the business of inspiring people.

Good stuff happens when you're in the people business. We promise.

The subtitle of this book is *Understanding, Sparking, and Sustaining Word of Mouth Marketing*. We could just as well substitute *Word of Mouth Marketing* with *Love and Passion*. Just promise you'll open your mind enough to embrace what we are about to share.

CHAPTER ONE

EVERY MARKETING PROBLEM IS A PEOPLE PROBLEM

Before we dig into understanding *why* word of mouth (WOM) matters, we want you to change your mind about the business you're in. Odds are you think you're in the marketing business. We're going to help you *unlearn* your marketing mindset and convince you that it's way more exciting and fun to be in the *people* business.

DITCH YOUR TITLE

First of all, shake the cobwebs from your brain and give yourself a new title.

Think: Chief People Officer. Chief Inspiration Officer. Chief Love Officer. Senior Manager of People Problems. Passion Conversation Facilitator. *Come on.* You can give back that Senior VP of Marketing title or that Brand Manager title as quickly as you received it. Or how about letting go of that social-media-something title? *You don't need it.* And if you are a CEO or a business owner and you hire marketers, make sure you are looking for people who love people. If you're in marketing, you're in the people business— and if you don't believe that core tenet, then stop reading. *Now.*

FORGET *MARKETING* PROBLEMS

**Companies face all sorts of *marketing* problems.
If they would reframe those issues as *people*
problems, their perspective would change.**

Reevaluating *your role* in solving these people problems makes it even more interesting. Consider the following people problems that leaders face:

- A company is suffering from sluggish sales growth because not enough people are buying.

- A business is experiencing low retention rates because not enough people are buying *repeatedly*.

- A brand reeling from poorly conceived products and programs doesn't have enough people truly interested in what they offer.

- An organization dealing with low engagement hasn't been able to make its cause relatable to people who can help them sustain support.

- A business hurting from unsatisfactory customer service must confront the problem of too many unhappy people.

If every marketing problem is a people problem, then every marketing solution must be people-based, right?
Oh, yeah. That's right.

EVERY MARKETING SOLUTION MUST FOCUS ON PEOPLE

The reasons are obvious: People buy products and use services. People make an unknown brand known. People work together to turn causes into crusades. It's *people* who form communities, talk, and share—and who fuel the engine of business. It's people who have the mouths that *word of mouth* refers to.

Steve Knox, former CEO of Tremor, Procter & Gamble's WOM marketing division, and currently a Senior Advisor with Boston Consulting Group, puts it well:

> I passionately, passionately believe that the world of marketing is moving to a relationship-based world. We in marketing have been trained to think about the consumer at arm's length . . . in an almost non-human way. And the new world of marketing is so much more about true relationships with people, which means there must be dialogue, and . . . conversation.

Steve is a leader in the WOM marketing industry, and we all need to listen when he talks. We take Steve's passionate words a step further and say:

IF YOU DON'T LOVE PEOPLE, GET OUT OF MARKETING—PERIOD

We're not saying you have be the kind of charismatic people person who makes friends with total strangers in elevators, but you do have to believe in and see the good in others. You have to believe this wonderful Earth of ours is full of amazing, beautiful people you'd love to know better. You should feel honored to spend time with your customers, not see them as a bother. You should feel driven to get to know them as people, not demographics or target markets.

We deal with marketing problems every day, which means we deal with people problems every day. Or perhaps a better way to say it is: We deal with people *opportunities* every day.

Anytime Fitness came to us with their problem: Not enough people are exercising at their gyms. The National Center for Family Literacy sought our guidance because not enough people understand that literacy goes way beyond reading and writing. DeVry University used our help to connect with its people (in their case, students) on 90 campuses and in over 70,000 homes. And Foundations Recovery Network (FRN) turned to us to help eliminate the stigma people associate with addiction. Those are very evident and *wonderful* people opportunities.

We've made a name for ourselves by igniting powerful, sustainable word of mouth movements for businesses and organizations of all sizes and design—big and small, for-profit and not-for-profit. These people-powered movements inspire people to buy, give, innovate, act, share, and most importantly, *talk*.

Our first book shared 10 lessons we learned about making movements happen. Since that book was published, we've connected with thousands of readers in person, over the phone, and, of course, online. We've had passionate debates about the ideas and real world case studies that our first book brought to life. We've continued to learn how to humanize a brand to spark deeper, more meaningful conversations between *people*.

These debates, discussions, and deep dives have led us to wholeheartedly believe that solutions to marketing problems are rooted in finding shared passions, igniting conversations, and creating community. You must have community before you can *ever* even begin to dream of a movement. And you know what moves conversation within a community to *advocacy*, the fuel for movements? *Passion*.

So, if you are ready to be in the people business—if you are ready to spark meaningful passionate conversations and find your advocates—repeat this mantra:

People are amazing. They form tribes. They create communities and social change. They make great discoveries. They struggle. They fall in love. They are social and emotional. They love to help others. They want to be a part of something bigger than their own lives. They want to change the world. As marketers (or *Chief Love Officers*), we'd be crazy not to tap into those strong desires. Connecting people through shared passions can lead to great things.

Okay, let's get back to the task of understanding WOM marketing by going back in history and getting to know a swell guy named Ernest Dichter.

LET'S REVISIT THE FUTURE OF WORD OF MOUTH MARKETING

The future of marketing happened way back in 1966 when Austrian-American psychologist Ernest Dichter published a long over-looked seminal article in the *Harvard Business Review*. Remarkably, this article was titled "How Word-of-Mouth Advertising Works," and its advice is just as relevant today just as it was back then.

Steeped in his in-depth research on consumer motivations, Dichter's article explained that consumers reject advertising messages because they are "more a sales tool than information and guidance." However, he contended, if people perceived a brand as a friend—and if the brand could project a voice to match—consumers would consider it to be more authentic and trusted, and the brand would be received with more enthusiasm.

Hmmm. Where'd that knowledge go for the last half-century?

Imagine how much further along we'd be if more marketers in 1966 had taken note of Dichter's smart findings on the importance of humanizing brands.

And just so you know, Ernest Dichter wasn't a fly-by-night shrink spewing cockamamie ideas. He's known as the "father of motivational research." According to a 1998 *New York Times* article, he "was the first to coin the term focus group and to stress the importance of image and persuasion in advertising." His pioneering research techniques and analysis changed the way that giants like Chrysler, Procter & Gamble, Exxon, General Mills, and DuPont sold products to consumers.

Dichter's advice to humanize the brand to connect better with people wasn't psychobabble. It was indispensable marketing advice then, today, and tomorrow, no doubt.

Dichter's personal story began on August 14, 1907, in Vienna, where he was born to a family of Polish and German immigrants. The Dichters were dirt-poor, and Ernest would always recall the poverty and starvation of his formative years and credit it with sharpening his awareness of the pleasures and comforts to be found in even the most basic and essential material goods.

According to the Ernest Dichter papers, from the age of 14 the budding psychologist and marketing guru "concentrated on earning money." He began by picking wild mushrooms and berries in the countryside, and selling them to grocery stores. He first became interested in marketing when he worked in his uncle's department store. He even introduced music into the store in an effort to soothe customers while they shopped. (*Think about that as you're listening to the background music playing while you walk through the mall!*)

Following university training in psychology and informal training in psychoanalysis, he moved to New York in 1938. In 1939 he sent a letter to six corporations in which he offered his understanding in psychoanalysis as a way to radically improve their marketing strategies. He got his first gig at Ivory Soap. The Ernest Dichter papers report that after conducting a slew of one-on-one in-person interviews, he learned it was not the smell or price or look or feel of the soap that mattered to consumers. Rather, it was something else that made a person choose one soap over another; to use Dichter's word, it was the product's "soul." He came to understand that every product has an image and that people buy products not merely for the purpose they serve, but also for the values the products seem to embody.

Dichter explained that our possessions are extensions of our own personalities and serve as a "kind of mirror which reflects our own image." (This quote comes from a 2011 article in *The Economist*.) Dichter showed a photograph in his 1947 book *The Psychology of Everyday Living* of a woman applying lipstick with the accompanying caption:

Cosmetics provide psychological therapy.

Dichter is absolutely right. Cosmetics *do* make women feel better about themselves. Why else would American women spend

$7 billion a year on makeup?* Why else would they talk to their friends, read countless online articles, and have conversations on social media about one product's superiority over another?

Even back then, Ernest grasped a simple truth we have come to understand even better today: In a world where technology has made it possible to connect more deeply and stay engaged with your customers, the focus should not be on a product's features and benefits. It's not about facts and figures. It's about understanding how a product *(or an organization)* fits into a person's life—and understanding how it makes them *feel*.

IT'S ABOUT THE PASSION CONVERSATION

**After digging around and unearthing more about
Ernest Dichter, we believe he would have agreed with
us on this statement: It's not about the product
conversation; it's about the passion conversation.**

Still not convinced your marketing department is in the people business?

MARKETERS DO NOT DECIDE WHAT GETS TALKED ABOUT—*PEOPLE* DO

Marketers wanting to tap into the power of WOM marketing to increase brand awareness, preference, and purchase eventually learn a fundamental truth. As Chief Inspiration Officers, you want to *inspire* others so they will talk passionately on your behalf. And studies clearly indicate word of mouth is the most powerful form of marketing. According to research from McKinsey &

---

*www.thegloss.com/2009/05/01/beauty/how-much-do-you-spend-on-makeup.

Company, word of mouth is responsible for up to 50 percent of all purchase decisions. Studies also indicate there are seemingly endless ways to spark conversations using word of mouth. Word of mouth research firm Keller Fay Group has been tracking the conversations people have about brands since 2006. In fact, they are the only firm that regularly monitors both offline as well as online word of mouth about products, services, and brands. According to their findings, advertising only prompts 22 percent of all conversations people have about brands, products, and services. However, the vast majority of word of mouth conversations, 78 percent of them, are sparked by something else. Which means that the playground for triggering word of mouth from customers about brands is *huge*. Even answering the phone can present a huge opportunity to create a talk-able, sharable experience. Call 864-676-9663 if you want to see for yourself. (Don't be scared; it's just us.)

Anything and everything a customer can interact with is an opportunity to spark a conversation. Every customer touch point is a possible talking point, and since people (*not marketers*) decide what gets talked about, it's up to Chief Love Officers to give people something to potentially talk about at every customer touch point.

Products alone will neither spark nor sustain conversations. Nor will programs, campaigns, services, and so on. It has always taken and will always take people.

CONVERSATION LEADS TO CONSIDERATION

When a brand, cause, organization, or product is a part of the conversation, then it's under consideration. Stats galore back that up. Not to overwhelm you, but we know marketers like data, and even though we are trying to convince you to jump over to the people business, we are going to share a few more of our favorite WOM marketing stats.

- The Keller Fay Group has found that Americans will mention specific brand names about 60 times every week in conversations with others. In a year, that translates to over 3,100 mentions of brands by the typical American.

- A Harris Interactive report reveals 71 percent of us believe reviews, opinions, and conversations from family members or friends have a "great deal" or "fair amount" of influence on our purchase decisions.

- From McKinsey & Company: The reliability of the impact word of mouth marketing has on business is based upon the irrefutable fact that recommendations from family, friends, and friends of friends have greater influence over our purchase decisions than any other form of marketing.

- Study after study confirms this irrefutable fact, including the 2011 Experian Digital Marketer report which tells us: "Despite consumer reliance on digital devices and Internet-provided information, the most influential element driving purchase decisions today is still word of mouth, followed by information from a website."

PEOPLE BELIEVE PEOPLE THEY KNOW AND TRUST

So you have to give people something to love and something they love to *talk* about. Here is one more nugget we repeat often about word of mouth: According to the Keller Fay Group, 90 percent of word of mouth conversations about brands happen *offline*.

Here's how Keller Fay's Ed Keller explains this to us: "Despite the tremendous attention people are paying to social media, and the meteoric rise in the number of people using it, the overwhelming majority of word of mouth (WOM) for brand-related conversation still takes place the good old fashioned way—face-to-face."

A brand-related WOM conversation is one where at least two people mention a specific brand name during the discussion. It might involve an outright recommendation like, "Sharpie make the best markers. You should buy one." Or, it might simply involve a mention of the brand by name: "Did you know Sharpie now makes a hot pink marker?"

SOMETIMES YOU WANT TO BE INVISIBLE AND INDESCRIBABLE

Word of mouth marketing can be invisible to the human eye, but not the heart. While you can't necessarily see when it happens, you can definitely *feel it*.

John knows Whole Foods Market. He once served as their director of national marketing. Although the grocery chain does not have a full-blown WOM marketing program, they're highly successful thanks to ongoing word of mouth from customers. And what Whole Foods Market does at the store level to get customers talking is invisible to most shoppers.

Shoppers do not feel like they're being marketed to because Whole Foods presents food as *theater*. While a trip to a conventional grocery store is a chore, a trip to Whole Foods Market is a chance to explore. Whole Foods *emotionalizes* the grocery shopping experience by appealing to all the senses. Its stores are spotless, merchandising displays are dazzling, and the smells are beyond compare. Shoppers are often encouraged to taste and sample. Whole Foods Market celebrates food like it is a theatrical production.

They also make it a point to educate their customers on the role natural and organic foods can play in helping them live happier, healthier, and more rewarding lives. The company believes it can cultivate loyalty by educating shoppers on the natural and organic difference. They use every opportunity to communicate that good food *feels* good.

The best word of mouth isn't a marketing tactic. It isn't a tweet, a status update, a viral video, or anything else you can find on a social media website. Nor is the best word of mouth a publicity stunt or something a company does to get some buzz for a day. The best word of mouth is how a company does business *every single day*.

The goal of any business should be to make word of mouth marketing operationally invisible. That is, it should be how a business does business not just one day, but every day.

On-going, long-lasting word of mouth is very difficult to incite and maintain. This is because too many marketers treat word of mouth as an output. In other words, they try to sustain and manage the conversation rather than treating it as an input—*starting and sparking* the conversation.

Whole Foods Market and a handful of other businesses understand that the best, longest-lasting word of mouth happens when a business operationalizes this approach by making it invisible to the customers' eyes—but not their hearts, minds, or wallets.

And they also get the notion of love and shared passions. Whole Foods loves their employees. All the way down from the

C-level to the front line, they hire people who love what they love. The store experience they've built is one they actually love themselves and in the process, they have attracted customers who love and share their same passions. Because of this, loving their customers is as easy as loving themselves.

Now, let's talk about how Whole Foods and another people-powered business, Starbucks, use social media *conversation* tools.

PROVIDE *MORE;* PROMOTE *LESS*

The brands that are nurturing meaningful relationships with customers online aren't interrupting them with promotional messages on Twitter or Facebook. Instead, brands like Whole Foods and Starbucks are using these platforms to provide customers with more information about products/services. The vast majority of Starbucks's and Whole Foods's tweets are directed at someone (starting with the @ symbol), which means that they're responding directly to a comment. These brands' Facebook pages aren't littered with promotional status updates. Instead, they're taking a moment to *make a connection* with customers by providing them specific information. This might not be the sexiest way to use social media, but it's been a very effective way for these companies to develop evangelical customers.

While we're on the topic of Facebook friends, now's a good time to mention that real friendship is a little bit magical. The other day a friend of ours who is new to our town made a simple observation about making new friends that got stuck in our hearts: 90 percent of a having a friend is being a friend.

We have a lot of discussion around here about engagement—what exactly does that mean, and how do you really measure *true* engagement within a community? So many brands and organizations still feel the number of Facebook fans or twitter followers is a sign of promising engagement. *They really do.*

The other day John stumbled on an interesting study by the Ehrenberg Bass Institute for Marketing Science at the University of South Australia, "Facebook Fans: A Fan for Life?" He sent the entire team this quick summary:

> The authors studied the "People Talking About This" (PTAT) measurement from Facebook between October and November 2011 to determine how many fans are engaging with the brand after the initial "like." Their findings reveal less than 0.5 percent of Facebook fans engage with the brands they are fans of during any week.
>
> Of the 200 brands they studied, only one had 2 percent of their fans engage with them during a seven-day period. *(Included in these 200 brands are "passion" brands, names like Nike, Chanel, Harley-Davidson, Jack Daniels, Louis Vuitton, Tiffany & Co., etc.)*
>
> Just 20 brands reached the 1 percent level of engagement from fans on any given week.
>
> The authors close by writing, "The real question is how cost effective is it for a brand to attempt to drive engagement if the most they can reasonably expect is that 1 percent of fans will engage?"

This makes us think that maybe we have it all backwards. Perhaps the thing we should be measuring is our own effort to *be* a friend? This is something the community management team takes very seriously at Brains on Fire. As brands and organizations, we need to ask: Are we putting 90 percent of our energy to being our customers' friends?

FROM ED KELLER

CEO of word of mouth research firm Keller Fay Group and co-author of *The Face-to-Face Book*

"It was interesting to learn that some of the best 'word of mouth marketers' don't actually think that's what they are doing, per se. We talked to companies like MillerCoors, General Mills, Kimberly-Clark, and Zappos, as well as agencies like Crispin Porter + Bogusky, Starcom MediaVest, and Universal McCann. Generally, we chose to do these interviews because their brands were having success at improving consumer word of mouth based on our own data from our ongoing TalkTrack® surveys. Yet few of the marketers believed they were actively doing 'word of mouth marketing.'

"The epiphany came for us when we realized that word of mouth marketing is really another term for 'great marketing.' Products and campaigns that stimulate conversation tend to be successful; those that don't tend to fail. In our view, all great marketing is in fact 'social marketing' because social influence is the key to driving behavior change."

So we've just talked about two big companies, Whole Foods and Starbucks, who both understand the power of loving people, talk-able touch points, and word of mouth. But what about the smaller companies, the ones that far fewer people have heard about?

MEET URSA MAJOR

"Ursa Major?" you might wonder. "What kind of name is *that?*"
For starters, it's a name that sparks a conversation and tells a
pretty cool story. Oliver Sweatman and Emily Doyle named their
company, one that handcrafts super, natural skin care products
for men, after the "Great Bear" constellation for a simple reason: When they moved from New York to Vermont they became
"fixated with the idea of bears." A lot of people questioned
the name. But as Oliver explains, "The term, Ursa Major has
some cool history around it. Ptolemy referenced it, as did Homer
and Shakespeare. It's impossible to miss on a clear night in the
northern hemisphere. It's been used by all kinds of folks over
the ages as a way to find true North. We have a big attachment
to the outdoors; it's one of the reasons we moved to Vermont.
I think people like us who have this affinity with nature find
something a bit mysterious and alluring about the name. It's kind
of romantic. We like to think the name appeals to modern-day
explorers—people who actually enjoy digging into a brand and
learning its back stories." Oliver and Emily are glad they trusted
their instincts to venture to Vermont and name their brand to
reflect their passions.

Geno Church is a big fan of products that are made in America.
He's crazy-passionate about it, really. In fact, this book would've
likely focused *entirely* on made-in-America brands had Geno been
the sole author. Geno is also the ultimate modern-day explorer,
constantly searching for new products and brands. He discovered
Ursa Major one night while sitting in front of his laptop at his
kitchen table. He ordered some of the products, and they arrived
a couple of days later in a hand-painted gift box. Inside there was
a *real* handwritten note thanking him for the order. Ursa Major
is a high-touch, emotional brand, and according to Geno, Ursa
Major's products also do a great job helping his skin stay happy

and hydrated. Geno shared his latest find with everyone in the office loudly and proudly.

KITCHEN TABLE PASSION

Oliver told us that he and Emily answer every single email they get *personally*, often staying up late at night sitting together at the kitchen table to make that happen. It might take them a couple of weeks, but they answer them all. "It's funny because many times we wish we had a restaurant or a café or retail store. We like engaging with people and we like making them feel happy." But they don't have a café or retail store; they do most of their business remotely over the Internet. Still they longed to bring "some of that hands-on love," like the kind you get in a little café or small retail shop to what they were doing. And answering email and sending handwritten thanks is part of how they do just that.

Oliver and Emily are branders and marketers and explorers and business owners. They're in the people business and they are definitely putting in the 90 percent effort to be a friend to their customers. And they're growing a business through sparking word of mouth in the process.

CHAPTER TWO

LET'S UN-GEEK A LITTLE SMART RESEARCH TOGETHER

We talked in Chapter 1 about why you must fall in love with the people you serve, and about how you can become famous for the people who love you and the way you love them. We went through some history and word of mouth (WOM) marketing research, and we shared our beliefs and some examples about why finding and uniting people through *shared passions* and experiences matter so much.

Now we're ready to learn exactly *why* people talk—the real research-proven reasons. If you understand *why* people talk, you have a far greater chance of sparking people to talk about how you fit into their lives. And then, you'll have a better chance of knowing how to *inspire* them to talk.

In addition to the research-proven reasons why people talk, we are also going to include some of our own heartfelt beliefs about the role passion plays in sparking conversations and creating advocacy. We've said it before but we'll say it again: *We're all in marketing grad school.*

The entire *world* is actually in one form of grad school or another, whether they know it or not. We're pretty sure you get it; after all, you're reading this book! With technology changing the way we connect and grow businesses daily, we all have to think like students. Not just any students, but those hyper-engaged, eager, wide-eyed students that sit at the front of the classroom—you know, the ones whose notes you wish you could get your hands on. We have to be engaged in lifelong learning, or we soon get left behind.

Last year, Geno and John started taking their grad school studies up a notch within the walls of Brains on Fire. Geno and John began finding and reading shiny, smart academic research about *why* people share. They started taking notes and drawing conclusions, and their own research began to make sense. They were making observations about the *work we were doing* and the *knowledge they were gaining*, and passing it along to others on our team. We killed a few trees as we passed around pink-highlighted, crumpled-edged, hand-scribbled versions of some really smart research. We could have emailed it to each other, but this research felt so important we wanted to hold it in our hands and study it *old-school style*.

Geno and John turned their findings into a presentation, which they first shared at the Word of Mouth Marketing Association (WOMMA) in May of 2012. By the time we submitted this book manuscript, they had put their presentation, titled "WOMology: Dumbing Down Smart Word of Mouth Research," online, where it had been viewed on SlideShare over 90,000 times. Something had obviously hit a chord among our business peers.

Hopefully, we've already convinced you that you're in the people business. Here is one other truth we hope you'll embrace: *The people business* (that thing some folks call marketing) *has the ability to touch and change lives in countless positive and meaningful ways.*

Studying *why* people talk and share is key to selling more products, igniting social change, and moving people to take action and become advocates and evangelists. So get your #2 pencils and highlighters out, and we'll share what we've learned and have come to believe.

THE WORD OF MOUTH OPPORTUNITY

We believe sparking word of mouth is a problem of know-*how*, not knowledge.

We already *know* what gets people talking. However, we're not sure about how to apply that knowledge.

Lots of great academic research exists to explain the science behind WOM marketing. And now we have available a large amount of research on why people share. This base of knowledge is super smart; however, it isn't readily accessible or easily understandable.

Most marketers today are confusing hindsight with foresight, and forgetting all about insight as they develop WOM activities.

Businesses are too fixated on mimicking best practices from other companies to become *their* company's next practice.

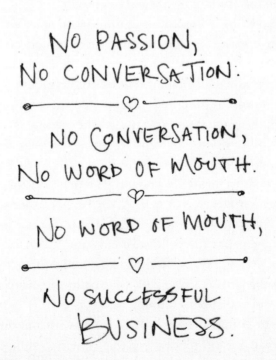

NO PASSION,
NO CONVERSATION.

NO CONVERSATION,
NO WORD OF MOUTH.

NO WORD OF MOUTH,

NO SUCCESSFUL
BUSINESS.

In other words, they've fallen victim to check-the-box marketing. Must get on Pinterest. *Check.* Must use Facebook to engage with customers. *Check.* Must Tweet fast and furiously. *Check.*

Too many people and organizations are putting the *what* before the *why* as they execute the *how.* They want to spark word of mouth with all their check-the-box marketing activities, but these conversations are not taking hold because a crucial ingredient is missing: *Passion.*

WHAT MOTIVATIONS SPARK CONVERSATIONS?

Academics have dug deeply into the science behind *why* people talk about brands. There's a trove of new research into the motivations behind WOM conversations. However, most of this research is cloaked with rigorous academic language that obfuscates understanding by ordinary people.

Despite its complicated nature, this new WOM academic research is something we all must strive to understand because it can play a very important role in how we design strategies and activities that spark and sustain conversations. In order for us to begin to use this research—and help others to do the same—we had to dig through the language to *un-obfuscate* the message. We rolled up our sleeves and translated all those $5 words and piles of numbers into some well-chosen 25¢ words (*and … well … still a few numbers*). Our hope is to make this knowledge more accessible so we can use it to create strategies that spark WOM conversations.

In 2011, the Marketing Science Institute published a thought-provoking paper titled "On Brands and Word of Mouth." The authors, Renana Peres, Ron Shachar, and Mitchell J. Lovett, put forth a theoretical framework to explain the motivations behind why people talk about brands.

We're going to layer this research with our in-the-trenches proof that passion plays a big role in why people talk. We have all known really shy people who come to life in a huge way when they discuss something they're passionate about. Passion takes the conversation up a notch. It motivates all of us to speak out in one way or another. *Passion tips conversation to advocacy.*

We took this complicated, heady stuff and distilled it down to its gist, which is:

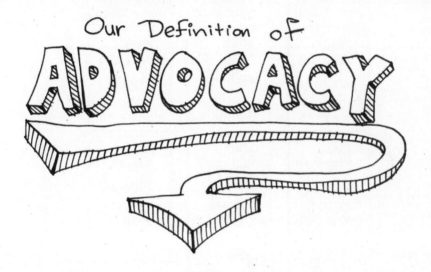

Our Definition of ADVOCACY

Advocacy occurs when people are inspired and empowered to share their love for an idea, cause, product, or brand, so much so that they become a living messenger for that idea, cause, product, or brand.

functional conversation

 social conversation

 emotional conversation

 functional newness

 social signaling

 emotional amusement

 functional complexity

 social uniqueness

 emotional anxiety

 social expertise

The Periodic Table of WOMology

 social passion

THERE ARE THREE MOTIVATIONS THAT SPARK CONVERSATIONS ABOUT BRANDS AND ORGANIZATIONS.

MOTIVATION #1

*People engage in Functional conversations about
brands to get information needed
to make decisions and to better interpret
the world around them.*

SHARE INFORMATION | *FACTUAL & FUNCTIONAL*

The most basic motivation for conversation is functional, one person sharing useful information with others. This allows people to make more educated decisions and better interpret the world.

The functional element explains why people share and seek knowledge about products, services, and the world around them. People have always relied on the power of WOM to understand new and complex things. New and complex things prompt us to talk to others about how, when, and where to use products that might be useful.

Here's a great example of a new service that has a lot of us talking—well, at least those of us who wear glasses. Warby Parker is righting a wrong—as they say, "Prescription eyewear simply should not cost $300+." They have also created an entirely new way to pick out affordable frames and lenses. It's a little bit complicated: You select five pairs online. All five frames are shipped to you (without prescription lenses) so you can try them on. You have up to five days to decide which ones you'll keep. Then, you ship all five frames back (with Warby Parker's prepaid return label), and wait for your prescription glasses to arrive.

You can also opt for a virtual try-on by uploading a photo and superimposing the glasses of your choice. You can even save the pictures or share them online to get feedback from your friends. There's a functional story to tell because it is an entirely *new* way to buy glasses.

Warby Parker also has a charitable promise: For every pair of glasses they sell, they donate a pair to someone in need. Not only have they created a smart company, but the four founders are also giving their customers a lot to talk about—and a lot to love.

HERE'S HOW PASSION FITS IN

One of Greg Cordell's passions is building things with his hands. He's a tinkerer. If you need to know what type of drill to use for a certain project, he's your man. Chances are he'll tell you his favorite *brand* of drill if you're thinking of buying one. If you happen to be near his house, he might walk over to the garage, bring out his favorite drill, and show you just how great it works and how cool it is.

Robbin Phillips is passionate about hot yoga, and it turns out that people have lots of questions about hot yoga. How hot is it? Is it harder than traditional yoga? What do you wear? Our advice: unless you *really* want to hear a whole lot of detailed answers, don't even get her started. She'll be picking you up at 5:30 a.m. to go to a class with her if you're not careful.

People who are passionate about something share functional information about that particular something often, and with a force that sticks. They share because they believe they're adding value to another person's life.

MOTIVATION #2

People engage in Social conversations about brands to impress others, to express uniqueness and to increase their reputations.

SIGNAL UNIQUENESS |
DISTINCTIVE & INTERESTING

A more involved motivation is at play when people signal their uniqueness through distinctive and interesting conversations and actions in social settings. Psychologists and biologists have a term for this; it's called social signaling. You are sending a social signal that you are unique.

Social signaling plays a significant role in driving word of mouth conversations. People will signal their individuality, expertise, and passions to society by talking about brands with which they uniquely identify.

Social signaling is a method of enhancing our sense of self. People often feel better about who they are by talking to others about preferences, hobbies, and even brands that are as distinctive and interesting as someone views him or herself to be.

According to Peres, Schachar, and Lovett in their academic study, "The higher the degree of differentiation of a brand, the easier it is for an individual to project uniqueness by engaging in word of mouth about it." In other words, brands like MINI (a car that is very unique in size and design) often signal a person's uniqueness. Geno's a huge MINI fan, and he will tell you, "Driving a MINI shows I care about my carbon footprint, I don't need a big fancy car to define me, and I love and appreciate great design." Geno talks about his love of MINI a lot. A whole lot.

We've all engaged in word of mouth conversations about brands that signal our uniqueness to others, often without even realizing it. When you see someone on the street wearing a Patagonia jacket and Tom's shoes sipping on a Starbucks coffee, you get a general impression about that person. Getting dressed every day is often an exercise in social signaling.

Social signaling turns us into connectors because we attract others to us who share our similarly unique passions.

HERE'S HOW PASSION FITS IN

Some people even go so far as to permanently tattoo a brand or cause on their bodies for the world to see. They want others to take notice of who they are and what they stand for. When you see someone with a Harley-Davidson emblem or an Anytime Fitness Fitness Rebel logo permanently inked on their body, it takes social signaling off the charts.

What drives people to proudly wear your logo on their clothes or mark their body with a tattoo on your behalf? We think the answer lies in finding the passion conversation and letting it shine. *You* have to get to that level of passion about what you are doing in order to inspire others to do the same. People have to know exactly what you believe in and what you stand for.

Most of John's friends view him as a beer expert. He loves to talk about craft beer and is always on the lookout for a willing set of ears. When he's with a group of friends at a bar, they ask him to make a recommendation. Some people even consider him a *beer coach*. Many of his friends will even go so far as to text him a photo of a beer menu to have him shoot back a recommendation. (Did we mention that he has a collection of hundreds of beers cataloged by type and stored at just the right temperature in his house?) And every time someone learns about John's love of beer in a social setting, it enhances his reputation and signals his uniqueness.

MOTIVATION #3

Brands that invoke strong Emotional feelings are more likely to be talked about.

When we are OVERJOYED, We TELL OTHERS

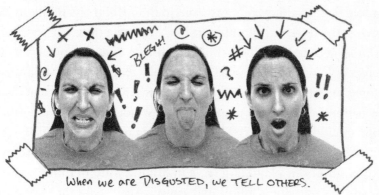

When we are DISGUSTED, we TELL OTHERS.

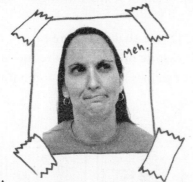

And when we are INDIFFERENT,
we DON'T TELL OTHERS.

SHOW EMOTIONS | *LOVE & HATE AND SHOCK & AWE*

People are more likely to talk about brands and organizations when they evoke strong, polarizing emotions on the edges of love and hate, or shock and awe.

"LIKE" IS NOT A BRAINS ON FIRE WORD

People engage in *emotional* conversations about a brand either because they're excited about something and love it, or they're disgusted by something and can't stand it. Brands and organizations that invoke strong emotions are more likely to incite these conversations. Think about it: We tell other people when we are overjoyed. We also tell people when we're appalled. We talk about things we love and things we hate, and we don't say much when we're indifferent about something. What's the point? We're just not passionate enough to talk about things we merely "like." *Like* is not a Brains on Fire word.

According to the "On Brands and Word of Mouth" academic paper, emotions play a large role in driving word of mouth. When a person experiences emotional arousal, they share the experience with others.

Studies have shown that high-arousal emotions like amusement and anxiety inspire more word of mouth conversations than low-arousal emotions like sadness and contentment.

HERE'S HOW PASSION FITS IN

Emotions often trigger passions. And passions become a part of who we are. They find their way into our conversations. Every time anyone from Brains on Fire speaks, we tell the story of Love146. And while you may have read about it in our first book, the work they do and the stories they tell are the kind that deserve to be repeated over and over.

Love146's growing community of abolitionists is an example of passionate, emotionally triggered sharing. Rob Morris and his team from Love146, which was formerly called Justice for Children International, came to us in 2007 with a problem. It seemed that a group of lawyers in Texas had trademarked the name "Justice for Children International," and Rob had until the end of that year to find a new name for his organization. After he told us his mission—to end child sex slavery and trafficking throughout the world—we knew we had to help him figure out what to rename this amazing group.

So Rob and some others on staff came to visit us. Upon sitting down together, the first thing we asked him was: Why was he doing this? The story that followed that question floored us. In Rob's words:

> In 2002, a small group of friends and I traveled to Southeast Asia to see what was going on firsthand. While there, we went with a couple of undercover investigators into a brothel posing as customers. Having to pose as the very thing we were so repulsed by was one of the most disturbing experiences of our lives.
>
> We found ourselves standing in a room looking through glass windows at little girls with red dresses on who were being sold as commodities. These girls were sitting there watching children's cartoons on little television sets. And we were standing shoulder-to-shoulder with men who

were purchasing these little children by number. They had numbers pinned to their little red dresses. These girls had even the dignity of a name stripped from them.

One of the most appalling things we encountered that night was the look in these children's eyes. There was nothing there—no life left. They were just staring robotically—blankly—at these crackling little television sets. I can distinctly remember one girl there, one who I guessed was probably new to the brothel because there was still a fight left in her eyes. She was the only one not looking at the television sets. She was staring out of the glass at us.

I don't know her name. I'll never know her name. But I'll never forget her number. Her number was 146. There was still a something in her eyes. There was still life left there.

As you can imagine, there wasn't a dry eye in that meeting. And from the telling of his story, we found the new identity for the organization: Love146.

Every time Rob, one of his team members, or one of us tells that story, it sparks a lot of emotions. People cry. They get angry. They tell others. They raise their hands to get involved. They give money. They go to the website to learn more. No one just *likes* or *dislikes* that story. They have an incredibly passionate reaction to it.

We have seen this story repeated over and over again, and it's been spread primarily through word of mouth. The website gets hundreds of thousands of hits a month and donations have risen. Other like-minded organizations have joined forces with Love146 to help raise awareness, and more people, including President Obama, are talking about the issue and taking action. It's definitely a passion conversation, just do a web search for

Love146 and you will find tons of images of people who have tat-tooed that nameless girl's number on their bodies.

KEEP EMOTION TOP OF MIND

Professor and author of *Contagious*, Jonah Berger, also found through his research that items we see often and in public spaces spark conversation. Its not just interesting stuff that gets talked about. Cheerios and Coke are two of the most talked-about brands in America, in part because they do have great products that people love, but in part because we see them all the time. It's been proven that visual cues spark conversation. So how can you use this knowledge to find ways to keep your passion, cause, product, or brand visible?

CREATE MEANINGFUL CONVERSATION TOOLS

One of the greatest conversation tools we've seen is a simple cloth patch with the red number 146 on it. No logo, just the number 146 in red. Like the one the little girl wore in Rob's story. Less is more when it comes to conversation tools. You have to fight the urge to tell your whole story on a tee shirt or pin or any-thing wearable. No one wants to be a walking brochure. You want something that invites a question or a conversation.

Thousands of people in a few short years have bought or worn the Love146 patch. These people send a social signal about their emotional involvement by wearing it on their book bag or sewing it on their clothing. The band Paramore wears it on their guitar straps and clothing, and tells this young girl's story every time they perform. Many of us at Brains on Fire travel and we often have the patch pinned to our backpacks or luggage. We all have stories of face-to-face conversations sparked by wearing her number.

A NOTE ABOUT THE POWER OF VISUAL CUES FROM ROB MORRIS, CO-FOUNDER OF LOVE146

"It still amazes us when we get photos of people who have honored her with a tattoo of 146 on their bodies. People driving down Route 146 see highway signs and remember her because her number is on it. They go to the trouble of stopping on the highway, taking a photo and sending it to us or posting it online. That number has so resonated with people that they send us photos of random license plates with her number on it. They share photos of their hotel room numbers if they are staying in room 146. The examples go on and on, but the message is the same: When you root your messages in the truth and tell powerful, emotional stories, you can visually trigger people to quickly remember that story. They will even find their own visual triggers and share those."

STORIES ARE EASIER TO REMEMBER AND SHARE

Love146 is also an example of the power of story. The fact that people are more likely to remember stories and share stories is not a new concept. It's pretty basic WOM knowledge. Facts and figure don't stick. Like authors Chip and Dan Heath informed us, *stories stick*. And here's why: We internalize stories. They become personal to us, because we can imagine experiencing them ourselves. When you hear the story of Love146, you can see yourself standing in that dark and dirty brothel looking through the window into that little girl's eyes. Honestly, it's hard to hear her story and *not* have a physical or emotional reaction.

Close your eyes for a minute and see if you can re-tell the story of Love146. Short, powerful stories stick.

ANOTHER WAY TO CREATE EMOTION AND SPARK WORD OF MOUTH? DISRUPT SOMEONE'S SCHEMA

Steve Knox, who shared his wisdom in Chapter 1 about marketers being in the people business, made a lasting impression on many of us when he spoke at our 2010 Fire Session on the power of disrupting schemas. Steve explained that one way to spark word of mouth is to create disruptive experiences. It works in this way: The brain uses *schemas*, which are essentially shortcuts that we (*often unwittingly*) use to help us quickly analyze and assess our environment. Steve pointed out that two things happen when you create a disruptive experience that doesn't fit into people's preconceived schemas:

1. They're forced to stop and think.

2. They're forced to talk about it.

The example Knox shared with us was the "Miracle on the Hudson" in 2009, where a US Airways flight crash-landed in the Hudson River. Steve showed us a picture of the front page of a Seattle paper that had a picture of the plane in the Hudson, with passengers walking on the wings into rafts that would take them to safety. Bet you can see that photo in your mind as you read these words. Think of all the schemas that were shattered with that one photo:

- When planes crash, they are destroyed. (The US Airways plane landed on water, and wasn't substantially damaged.)

- When planes crash, people die. (No one died from the Hudson crash.)

- People don't walk on water. (The photo shows them walking on the wings of the plane, and it appears as if they are walking on water.)

Many years later we're still talking about the Hudson airplane crash because the outcome was unexpected. It challenged all the above schemas, and forced us to think *and* talk about what was happening.

This doesn't *always* work, and the disruption still has to appeal to ideals about the brand, person, or idea that we believe to be true, or that could be true. For example, Las Vegas tried to rebrand itself as a family-friendly vacation destination a few years ago. That's disruptive, but since the message wasn't consistent with what people believe to be true about Las Vegas, it didn't register. Another example was Diet Coke offering a version with vitamins. This was also disruptive, but didn't work because people don't consider Diet Coke to be a healthy drink, and don't buy it for health reasons.

As Knox explained, the disruption has to be "faithful to the foundational truths" of the brand in order to be effective. He cited an example from his Procter & Gamble days of a deodorant that was activated by moisture whose product claim was, "The more you sweat, the better you smell." That statement disrupts our normal way of thinking and gets us talking about the product.

So how can your business create something disruptive?

1. **Figure out what your brand or business's foundational truth is.** If you don't know, ask your customers.

2. **Ask yourself what schemas are already at play.** What do customers already think about you and your brand or organizations? What are their preconceived notions?

3. **What would disrupt those schemas?** What would make people stop, think, and talk about you?

4. **Are there blends that would make sense?** Can you play existing schemas about your brand off each other?

5. **So how do you get started?** You listen to your customers, remain open to schemas other than your own, and test and verify your results.

Knox also shared this wisdom with us that day: "Victory in marketing doesn't happen when you sell something, but when you cultivate advocates for your brand." He thinks disruptive schemas are at the core of why conversations start, but a disrupted experience alone will not get you *advocacy*. There must be a relationship associated with that disruption or the advocacy will not spread.

PASSION TIPS CONVERSATION TO ADVOCACY

Remember this line from Chapter 1? Let's take this earlier statement and mash up some of our thinking with Knox's wisdom.

> **Shared passions help *form relationships* that move conversation (*word of mouth*) to *advocacy*.**

And since we're studying some academic stuff, let's review:

- People are motivated to talk for functional (share information), social (publicly expresses uniqueness), and emotional reasons (delighted or disgusted).

- We talk about things that are in front of us, things we see often and in public settings.

- Visual cues work best when they invite a conversation.

- Stories make things sticky, easy to remember and repeat.

- When our normal patterns of thought are disrupted, we talk.

Conversation (*word of mouth*) has more impact when it's coming from someone you have a relationship with, and who's very passionate about the subject.

NOW, HERE'S WHERE ALL THIS ACADEMIC LEARNING GETS REALLY INTERESTING

The reasons we share offline are *completely different* from the reasons we share online, according to the "On Brands and Word of Mouth" study. Emotion is the main reason behind our face-to-face conversations, which we know tend to be more intimate. And we are more apt to share our emotions like excitement and anxiety when we're in the same room with another person *(or even on the phone)*. We are also very likely to share functional nuts and bolts information about brands face-to-face. Interestingly, we are less likely to signal our social uniqueness face-to-face because most of these conversations are intimate, and not of a broadcast nature.

When we're online, of course, we're often "broadcasting" to people out in the open on social networks. Because these conversations are in the open, online word of mouth is used more as a channel to socially signal our uniqueness to online friends and followers. Factual and functional information is the second trigger behind why we share online. While emotion is the main driver of our face-to-face conversations, it's the least likely driver of our online conversations. It's far more difficult for us to express a full range of emotions using words online rather than speaking words with physical expressions in face-to-face conversations. The tonality of our emotions gets lost in translation when we write how we feel and that's why it's the least likely trigger of our online conversations.

OFFLINE MOTIVATION

GOOD   BETTER   BEST

ONLINE MOTIVATION

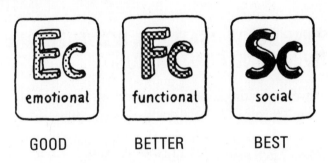

GOOD   BETTER   BEST

THIS LEADS US TO ASK THE QUESTION: CAN THE CONVERSATION *CHANNEL* ITSELF—WHETHER ONLINE OR OFFLINE—SHAPE WHAT PEOPLE TALK ABOUT?

There are so many ways to have a conversation these days—on a blog, by email, on the phone, in person, by text, in reviews on forums, tweeting a comment, posting pictures on Instagram ... *we could go on and on.* All those places present opportunities to connect as humans, and to give or receive word of mouth recommendations.

ANOTHER IMPORTANT POINT ABOUT ONLINE CONVERSATIONS: THEY ARE INTERMITTENT AND SPORADIC

The conversations we have with people on Facebook, Twitter, blogs, and through texting happen in spits and spurts. This means that we can think (or at least most of us do) before we respond. People have time to select and craft what they say, and give some thought to how they can be more interesting. And research shows we tend to talk online about products that are more interesting. Therefore, if your goal is to have people engage in more online conversation, you need to tell interesting, surprising, and awe-inspiring stories.

OFFLINE CONVERSATIONS, HOWEVER, ARE FLOWING AND CONTINUOUS

When we're speaking to someone in person or on the phone, there is less time for us to be selective about our conversation topics or comments. We tend to talk about what is right in front of us. Think about how often we discuss subjects like the weather or a restaurant. The weather is always a visual constant in our lives, and food cues are all around us causing us to talk about food *a lot* when we are face-to-face. If your goal is to get more meaningful face-to-face conversation, then you want to find a way to create conversation tools and triggers. We'll explore examples in the love stories to come.

WHEN DOES CONVERSATION BECOME ADVOCACY?

Saying "Geez, I wish I had a Coke" when we see someone walking by with one in their hands is one kind of word of mouth that matters for brands. But why do people *advocate* on behalf of a brand?

What moves it from conversation to advocacy? What makes Greg go out of his way to show you the brand of drill he loves so much and why? What creates a *lifetime customer*? We all know people who are so loyal to a brand that they would never switch. How can we go from being that brand people mention in passing to one that they *love*? How can we help our advocates find us and connect with us?

PEOPLE TALK ABOUT THINGS THEY ARE PASSIONATE ABOUT

On a scale of 1 to 10, people talk about and go out of their way to advocate on behalf of their 9's and 10's. This is the whole premise for the Net Promoter Score's effectiveness, a tool we often recommend to our customers.

A lot of companies and organizations will tell you that it's all about relationships, but those are just silly, empty business buzzwords unless you're ready and willing to take the time to understand your customers' passions and connect them to your organization's shared passions.

Finding shared passion is one of the greatest tools to developing meaningful relationships and sparking word of mouth.

Guy Kawasaki writes in his book *Enchantment* about two social scientists whose studies found the best negotiators spend 40 percent of their preparation time finding shared passion between the parties involved in the conflict.

Do you invest this much time with your employees (and yes, it often starts with your employees), your advocates, your customers, your donors? How do you find the shared-passion conversations that are true to who you are as a company?

You listen.

And as we implored in the previous chapter, don't dare ask, "What is your passion?" Nor should you look at data and

HOW THE NET PROMOTER SCORE WORKS, STRAIGHT FROM THEIR WEBSITE

"The Net Promoter Score, or NPS, is based on the fundamental perspective that every company can divide its customers into three main categories: Promoters, Passives, and Detractors.

"Asking the simple question: 'How likely is it that you would recommend [your company] to a friend or colleague?' allows you to track these groups and get a clear measure of your company's performance through your customers' eyes. Customers respond on a 0-to-10 point rating scale and are categorized as follows:

- *Promoters (score 9-10) are loyal enthusiasts who will keep buying and refer others, fueling growth.*

- *Passives (score 7-8) are satisfied but unenthusiastic customers who are vulnerable to competitive offerings.*

- *Detractors (score 0-6) are unhappy customers who can damage your brand and impede growth through negative word of mouth.*

"To calculate your company's NPS, take the percentage of customers who are Promoters and subtract the percentage who are Detractors."

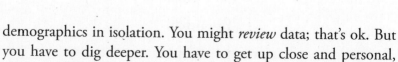

demographics in isolation. You might *review* data; that's ok. But you have to dig deeper. You have to get up close and personal, observe and participate in customers' lives. You go to their parties.

You share a meal with them or rebuild a car or go fishing all day. A storyteller friend of Brains on Fire said, "Give me a day, a boat, and some fishing gear and I can tell you anyone's story." You have to love your customers so much you *want* to go to dinner with them. You don't mind spending a day with them.

You have to connect as humans.

HOW TO MAKE THE MOST OF THE LOVE STORIES YOU ARE ABOUT TO HEAR

In the next four chapters we are going to let you inside the walls of Brains on Fire, and share four stories that are full of humanity and passion and love. While creating these strategies with our customers we didn't hold up the academic research we've just shared with you as a guideline, but we do believe you can see them at play. We are truly grateful to have connected with some of the most amazing and courageous people on the planet—our customers and their customers—and we don't take lightly the work they have allowed us to be a part of.

Each story is full of lessons learned. Ed Keller and Steve Knox will also give you their takeaways at the end of each story. Ed has a word of mouth researcher's perspective and Steve has worked on some very big brands, helping them spark word of mouth. We believe you'll gain a lot from their insights.

In an effort to help you apply those takeaways to your business, we're going to give you three possible assignments (called *Passion Explorations*) to do with other people inside and outside of your organization. Please go beyond the marketing silos for these assignments and instead seek out people who have contact with your customers. In fact, grab your customers themselves. Put them in a room together. Have fun. Laugh. And keep in mind that while working with real people and emotions is wonderful work, it can get messy—so embrace messy; it's okay. Take photos and send them to us. There are no right or wrong answers. Our hope is that we will help you to get outside of your normal marketing grooves and find new ways to touch lives, celebrate people, fall in love, discover passions, have fun, and grow your business in the process.

BE OPEN TO FINDING YOUR CAUSE

By the way, it's interesting to note that of the four stories we're sharing from four different companies, only *one* company is a not-for-profit, even though they all four feel very cause related. This reflects something we know for sure: It is possible for both for-profit businesses and not-for-profits to find their cause, and in the process, find their purpose, their *why*, and their passion conversation.

CHAPTER THREE

ADDICTION IS AN EQUAL-OPPORTUNITY EMPLOYER

I was wrong, just so wrong. I believed addicts were people who didn't have self-control. They were poor, had no loving family, and lived in tough urban areas. I would read stories in the paper about an overdose death and think, "I'm so happy that *my* son Andy will never be an addict. *My* son is a happy, straight-A student who is an artist and violinist, lives in a nice home, and has two loving parents. He even won first place in the D.A.R.E. essay contest!" And I thought it was all because I provided such a good environment for my son. What a great parent I was! My attitude was pompous, incredibly naïve, and judgmental. It was a fantasy world, a world in which many people live.

Andy's dad and I buried our only child on February 18, 2011 at the tender age of 22. He died of a heroin overdose.

—Pam Katchuk, www.heroesinrecovery.com

TODAY'S WORLD IS A CONNECTED WORLD

In a comfortable, suburban home in Raleigh, North Carolina, Pam Katchuk sat at her computer and typed the words "volunteer and stigma" into Google. That's how she discovered the Heroes in Recovery community, which led to her becoming a guest blogger on the website, and later a lead advocate for the movement. Lee Pepper, the Chief Marketing Officer of Foundations Recovery Network (FRN), met Katchuk in person for the first time at an advocate retreat in Nashville in February of 2013. (FRN's well-known dual-diagnostic treatment facilities include The Canyon in Malibu, Michael's House in Palm Springs, La Paloma in Memphis, and an outpatient facility in Atlanta.) At that meeting, Pam told the story of how she had lost her son Andy almost two years ago to the day.

Spend even a tiny bit of time with Lee and you'll most likely hear stories about his *own* two boys, his beautiful wife, or his love of running. You're almost sure to also hear his heartfelt personal and professional mission. He repeats it often and with a force that sticks: "Twenty-three million people each year need help for addiction; only 3 million actually seek treatment. We're looking for the other 20 million."

We have to break the stigma.

Like Pam, Lee believes with all his heart that the overwhelming stigma often associated with addiction and mental illnesses is what stops those other 20 million from reaching out for help. That stigma is what kept Pam in denial at times about her own son. "I now know that I didn't *want* to believe that Andy was taking drugs," Pam writes on her first blog post on December 26, 2012. She assumed, as she admitted later, that overdoses happen to other people who were "poor, had no loving family, and lived in tough urban areas." She was wrong.

While Andy's Mom and Dad were struggling with their son's health in 2010, Lee and his marketing team happened to see Geno Church speak at a Social Fresh conference in Nashville. "We were missing something and on to something at the same time," says Lee, "and Geno's stories of the Love146 movement to end child sex slavery helped put some words around some of the thoughts we were having at Foundations Recovery Network."

Society likes labels, and these labels deter many people— especially those afflicted with disease—from reaching out for assistance and treatment. For years, people afflicted with AIDS suffered needlessly due to the shame associated with the disease. They felt that it was just too painful to admit the truth. When perceptions change, an amazing thing happens: *progress*.

This is something Lee understands very well: "When former first lady Betty Ford passed away, we held an internal meeting where we read her obituary and discussed her impact on behavioral health. She had 'come out' with her struggles with alcoholism in 1976. Two years prior to that, she had openly shared her struggles with breast cancer. It really made an impact on us to look at how breast cancer and seeking treatment became a national movement—and how not much progress has been made in creating a movement to get treatment for addiction or to break the stigma associated with it. During those 40 years, those two medical issues went on two completely different paths.

It's true. Think about it. Studies have found that helping employees recover is more cost effective than termination, yet some employers believe that firing an employee with a drinking or drug problem is a lot easier than providing or facilitating rehab. Can you imagine the protest that would erupt if employers treated workers with cancer or heart disease the same way? Insurance companies get away with refusing to pay for alcohol or drug treatment, or with charging higher deductibles and co-pays than for treating any other disease. People who need the help for addiction for families with loved ones who are addicted are often afraid to speak up. They hide in shame. And that's created a big mess.*

Lee continues, "A lot of the social ills we have stem from shame. People forget how far breast cancer awareness—and cancer awareness in general—has come. I heard an interview with comedian Bernie Mac years ago on Howard Stern. He was talking about how when he was a child in the 70s, his mother went away for six weeks—and he was just told she was 'away.' She was actually in the hospital having a double mastectomy. But you didn't talk about that back then. Getting breast cancer was a shameful thing—like she had done something wrong."

"This is 2013!" Lee exclaims, "Why are we still repeating the same mistakes that we learned from these other social movements? We have got to take action now. We *must* be able to talk about addiction and the mental illness that often comes with it openly and without shame, or else we're still going to have not only thousands of people each year dying from this disease, but also impacting millions of lives needlessly … in a negative way."

Lee's stories create an anxiety about the injustice and trigger *emotional* conversation inside and outside of FRN's walls.

We have to reach "the other 20 million."

FRN hired Brains on Fire to help them find a way to talk *with*—not *at*—people struggling with addiction. We started the process by visiting each of FRN's residential and outpatient centers and talking to the clinical staff as well as the cooks, therapists, and call-center teams. What struck us was how much everyone *cared*—and *care* is actually an understatement. These people were *passionate* about their goal to help people struggling with addiction. In fact, many of FRN's employees are in recovery themselves.

---

*www.hbo.com/addiction/stigma/52_coping_with_stigma.html.

They are living the better lives they are helping others find. Their work is actually part of their recovery.

Since people often turn to search engines online in times of need, FRN's marketing task was simple and clear: Be at the other end of that search. With solid information and a big, bold phone number. We found out in listening in on the calls at the call center that come in from these various "content driven websites" that the marketing team produces, that FRN has a "spider web" network. This means that if an employee can't provide the right solution for the person on the other end of the line, then they'll find someone in their vast and interconnected network of addiction and health care specialists who *can* help. Every person who works at FRN understands that these callers are searching for real people with real information—and when someone is reaching out for help, you don't let them go.

We began to wonder if we could create an online community of real people to help those struggling to find answers. Could we speak powerfully with people, *through* people? Could we help moms who were finally facing the truth that the marks on their son's arms *are* heroin tracks, or help daughters who are desperately trying to save a parent? Could we support someone who is taking that first, tentative step after realizing they have a problem that's gotten out of hand? Could we create a *functional* tool for people to *share and seek* information? How could FRN reach the other 20 million, and, more importantly, give those who *love* and care for them a place to step into a meaningful conversation that would break the stigma of addiction?

When we first met FRN's marketing team, they were exploring the role loved ones play in a person's decision to get help. They had just created and were beginning to run a series of television spots that recognized the family members of those in recovery as heroes, and it was hitting an emotional nerve. Individuals working towards recovery themselves are often called heroes for their brave choices and hard work, and rightfully so. But aren't their supportive family members and loved ones heroes as well? Don't *they* deserve to be recognized and empowered as well?

Imagine what could be.

Together with the team at FRN, we started dreaming. We know that addiction doesn't just affect those with the addiction—not by a long shot. Most of you reading this book can likely tell stories of addiction's strong impact in your own lives. Could we engage new, provocative, informed conversations outside of those seeking treatment? Could we inject new perspectives, ideas, and expressions into the mainstream? Could we make *recovery*, not addiction, the newsworthy topic? Could we break the stigma associated with addiction by celebrating the everyday heroes affected by this disease: the dads, the sons and daughters, the neighbors next door? Could we create a new voice of hope and recovery with a quilt of shared stories and a community called Heroes in Recovery?

THE HEROES IN RECOVERY COMMUNITY BEGINS INTERNALLY

We went back to the core groups at FRN, who helped us capture such meaningful insights, to celebrate how their involvement could bring the idea of Heroes in Recovery to life. First, we made a plan to share the word of mouth marketing strategy internally with each of the facilities' leaders. We invited people within FRN to share their own stories online and with each other. We needed them to help us find hand-raisers, people who were powerful in recovery and willing to share their journey with the world.

We also created an identity mark for the community that reflects real-life, heroic stories. Greg Ramsey from Brains on Fire and the FRN team poured themselves into finding six stories from FRN alumni and even from people they stumbled upon online who were bravely sharing their personal tales of recovery.

Greg speaks so quietly and thoughtfully you have to lean in to hear him at times, but every word is fueled by passion: "As a designer, I began to see that the word *heroes* could take on a life of its own. Each letter represents a real person's story. I got to speak personally with people who were struggling with addiction or had come through it and were on the other side. Some had a loved one in the process of recovery. I helped them highlight the parts of their journey that were most important. I tried to take those meaningful events and mold them into something you could look at and touch and feel. These people became so very real to me in the process. And personally, I was at a place in my life where recovery had touched my family. The process of designing the Heroes logo—[one] that told real stories about people in recovery or who were touched by recovery—helped me make sense of what my own family was experiencing."

THE JOURNEY BOX

The passion inside an organization has to match the passion outside. Heroes in Recovery is an internal movement as much as an external movement.

Greg continues on with the story of how Heroes in Recovery began to evolve and come to life within the walls of FRN: "The idea for the Journey Box grew out of our visits to the facilities. We saw staff encouraging patients to keep a visual journal of their recovery. Everyone also saw the beauty and the magic of the letters logo, and witnessed firsthand how capturing visuals could help people express their stories. We created a beautiful box that

FRN could use at their treatment centers. Now when someone arrives at a center, they receive a Journey Box. They use it to collect pictures and other little things to help them chronicle their own journey to recovery—capturing where they have been, and, most importantly, where they are going. Making it visual in this way seems to help them talk about it differently—and honor their journey in a different way."

The Journey Box is a tangible and physical reminder of someone's heroic journey of recovery. It's a keepsake that each person can fill with anything and everything that is a part of their story: photos, reminders of good days, bad days, a good luck charm, a letter, a rock, a key—anything that helps them tell the world about their journey to recovery. We used this conversation tool internally with staff and patients to inspire and celebrate stories that they could share, not just in person, but also online at www.heroesinrecovery.com.

"To me the Journey Box was a big key," Lee says. "Being able to tie these stories and this effort to our actual treatment model isn't something we've been able to accomplish overnight. But it's crucial to the staff to see how we can and are integrating the Heroes community into the company. The Journey Box allows us to build a bridge between the clinical work that is being done and this community, this social movement called Heroes in Recovery. It's important that Heroes doesn't just sit as some website off to the side that we support. We are *integrating* it into our company's culture. In one of our early internal meetings, where we emphasized the need to bring this community to life, one of the clinical staff from Florida was present. She was cutting magazine pictures out and gluing them to her Journey Box. She then told those of us in the room her story, which is so powerful. People were crying." Lee takes a long breath and searches for just the right words, "Okay, here we go. Now we are really connecting everybody."

LEAD THE WAY

What is a hero? A man or woman distinguished by exceptional courage, strength, and fortitude; someone who fights for a cause.

Who is a hero? A client. A parent. A therapist. A friend. A sibling. A treatment facility. You. Me. Them. Us.

Those words are in our initial presentation to the FRN leadership team. We believe strongly that a community must be in place before you can ever ignite a movement or create social change. And all great communities (and movements) have leaders to guide the conversation. We poured a lot of discussion and a lot of thought into how we might find the right leaders, the original six heroes, for the Heroes in Recovery movement.

Lee remembers approaching the search carefully: "We were a little concerned that we were going to put out this call for Advocates and were going to get a lot of people who wanted to help and we could only choose so many. We didn't want people to feel like if they weren't selected they had done something wrong. We also wanted to go beyond our own foundation alumni to represent an even broader voice of recovery."

The first six lead advocates, Sue, Vanessa, Sean, Jordan, Sidney, and Nate, were hand selected. After an intense and emotional training session in Nashville, they began sharing their personal stories of recovery. Those six very diverse advocates were the starting point for over 300 other people to share their voice of recovery online within a year's time.

ANONYMITY IS NOT SECRECY

That first year's number of shared stories (and the people who have since engaged with those stories) might seem low to some, but for Heroes, it's real and solid progress, especially given the stigma and secrecy surrounding addiction. Since 1936, when Alcoholics Anonymous first shared *The Big Book* of 12 steps as a path to recovery, anonymity has been upheld and honored as a key covenant.

"I think we have been confused about what anonymity means," Lee says. "We have come to understand it as meaning *secrecy*. But we are challenging the whole notion of secrecy with Heroes. One of our leads in this last training retreat in Nashville shared her feeling about this as we went around the room sharing stories. She said, 'This is my second year being involved as a lead advocate and I have been conflicted at times because of my relationship with AA, NA, and Alanon.' But she went on to say, 'I have come 180 degrees.'"

"We were so happy to hear that. We could feel a certain hesitation from her in our weekly advocate calls at times. When she announced her 180-degree shift, I realized we can't reach everybody in the same timeframe, and that's okay. It's taken other people six months; and there are people within our own walls who still don't get the importance of talking openly. And that's all right because we will get to them eventually."

Ask me about my Journey.

In addition to the Journey Box, we also created buttons and palm cards that staff and advocates use to start offline conversations. These conversation tools don't attempt to tell the whole story of Heroes in Recovery; however, they create enough visual interest to spark a question. Buttons with just one of the beautiful logo letters on them or invitations to "Ask me about my Journey" were all developed with a single purpose in mind: to spark a face-to-face, meaningful conversation. These tools empower people in recovery to quietly send a social signal that they are part of the Heroes in Recovery movement. We believe that social signaling at its best is done quietly.

THERE'S POWER IN JUST BEING THERE

In order to break the stigma of addiction and celebrate our growing community of Heroes in Recovery, we knew we had to hit the road and present the message in person at a broader community level. As we stated previously, 90 percent of all brand conversations take place offline—and we don't take that fact lightly. In order to reach "the other 20 million," FRN knew that Heroes couldn't be just a website.

FRN created the Heroes in Recovery 6K races to serve as an educational tool for the community at large, and to remind individuals that while they are on a personal journey of recovery, they aren't going it alone. Many others are on that road with them. We *disrupted the norm* of 5K races and introduced a 6K race for Heroes in Recovery. The number six is meaningful, not only because it represents the six heroic lives woven into the word *heroes*; it also underscores the significance of pushing yourself just a little bit harder and propelling oneself just a little bit further down the road to recovery.

FRN's inaugural 6K was held in 2011 on a racecourse in Leiper's Fork, Tennessee, during the month of September, National Recovery Month. It was sold out with 250 participants and around 100 volunteers. Since then, FRN has organized a number of successful races across the country, and the number of races and participants continues to grow.

It's hard to measure how many lives are touched and conversations sparked by the 6K races across the country. Most of the conversation takes place quietly between two or three people. Greg Ramsey and his family participated in a Heroes race held in a park in Greenville, South Carolina. A man who happened to be walking in the park that morning approached Greg after the race to ask what the race was for. After Greg explained the Heroes in Recovery movement, the man revealed that he was in early recovery himself and just getting back on his feet. He seemed anxious to connect with someone, so Greg gave him a palm card with the Heroes web address and invited the man to share his story and join the community. "I don't know his name," says Greg, "and I will never know where that simple conversation led or the impact it had on his life. But I know it would have never happened if FRN wasn't there that day."

In addition to raising awareness, each race raises money that's given to a local charity. Greg and his family also attended a 6K race in Boulder, Colorado, that gave proceeds to Phoenix Multisport, an organization that supports people recovering from addiction by providing them with a sober community to take part in physical and social recreation. Members of Phoenix Multisport came out en masse for the Heroes 6K.

Greg remembers the day: "It's cool to see people cheering each other on, becoming fans of each other. These races really create a real sense of community for a day. They are also symbolic of recovery itself, and capture what it's all about. It's hard work, and everyone is participating at different levels. Some are walking. Some are running fast. But no one is alone. I also loved that the race gave a platform for a local group to be an inspiration to their community. It was amazing to hear the leader of Phoenix Multisport tell his group's story and connect with others in such a meaningful way."

As Greg points out, the 6Ks are perfect metaphors for the road to recovery: a group of individuals moving at different paces but supporting one another and cheering each other on toward a common goal.

The 6Ks are just one example of events that are bringing the Heroes movement face-to-face with broader communities. FRN is open to all types of events that help spread the word. "We had a guy visit us from Santa Monica," says Lee. "We were talking about Heroes and he told us that he wanted to hold an event. And I asked, 'Do you want us to organize a 6K in Santa Monica?' He said 'Well, what about a surfing competition?' So we are going to do a surfing competition in Venice Beach in October. That's the model for Heroes. People have different passions and talents. If you want to do an art night, like we did in Memphis, if you want to do a trivia night like we did in Nashville, if you want to do a surfing competition, let's do it! And you can do it with the goal of growing the Heroes in Recovery community. We can reach so many people that way."

Share it with Sean.

In his early twenties, Sean Morrison was one of the youngest of the original six Advocates selected for Heroes in Recovery. He told his story of recovery in his first blog post, which he ended with these final remarks:

> I share my story in hope that maybe, just maybe, I can help one person overcome this disease of addiction. There is hope, there is recovery, and there is an awesome life to be lived. I am living proof. I am a Hero.

One exciting sign of word of mouth–powered momentum becomes evident when ideas to grow a community start emerging from the community itself. In the summer of 2012, Sean had an idea. What if he hit the road on his summer vacation from college and captured 60 heroic stories in 30 days? He presented the concept to FRN, and together we helped Sean bring his idea to life. He started in New York and zigzagged across the country to his final destination in Nashville. It was a remarkable journey, and the 60-plus stories he captured in person were nothing short of amazing, including the one that follows.

CONNECTIONS ARE A POWERFUL FORCE

Greg and his family met and made fast friends with Sean at the 6K in Colorado while he was doing his road trip across the states. Sean met a man at that same race named Tarr, with whom he had the following inspiring interaction:

> When I first saw Tarr, he was talking to a young man who was thinking about taking the frightening leap of recovery. The tone of the conversation is one I will never forget. He told the young man a bit about his background and that he was there if he needed anything. He showed love and care.
>
> Tarr started off telling me he grew up in a family where many of his relatives were members of law enforcement. He always felt like the black sheep of the family, not knowing how to fit in or act around family and others. He was addicted to methamphetamine and other drugs at 16, and ended up running with a gang, causing him to be in and out of prison for multiple crimes. His lying, stealing, robbing and drug addiction lasted for 16 years until he found meditation, prayer, and became active in a sober community.
>
> His hope for a better life started when he moved to Colorado and tried to detox from drugs. Tarr relapsed after trying to get clean—and it was at that point that he realized he was going to have to put as much work into recovery as he did into using drugs.
>
> Tarr picked himself up and got involved in a 12-step program, but that was not enough for him. He had to get active. This is when he found Phoenix Multisport,

a sober active living community. He got involved in climbing, boxing, biking, and many more sports. He also practiced more meditation and prayer to draw him closer and stronger in his sobriety.

It was amazing hearing him talk about his experience with helping others. As mentioned above, the first time I saw Tarr he was talking to a young boy about getting sober. I asked Tarr, "What is it like talking to others or young people who are seeking recovery?" He said, "I like to think of people in recovery as gems, they are true gems because we were dirty man, we were like that rock sitting there, all dirty, nasty and rough. But you take a little grit and sand and polish it, and these people become true walking and talking miracles—true gems."

—heroesinrecovery.com/stories

In order to help more people, we have to grow and open more facilities.

FRN is a for-profit business with a very purpose-driven, lofty goal: to break the stigma of addiction and mental illness so that more people—"the other 20 million"—will seek help. They have to continue to grow and be profitable as an organization to make that goal a reality. And like every organization, they have to spend their marketing dollars wisely, and see a return on investment.

HOW DO YOU MEASURE SUCCESS?

"A lot of companies struggle with how they measure." Lee says. "I wasn't going to let the inability to provide our board with real numbers stop me though. People nowadays often get caught up in the sex appeal of social media and the web. But before you go rolling down a path, you need to establish what your metrics are and figure out how and what to measure."

Lee continues, "We have been really fortunate in that regard. One simple thing we look at is Facebook engagement. The Heroes page is growing at three times the rate of any of our facilities' pages, which is a clear testimony to the fact that people are more likely to identify with a social movement than they are with a business.

"We have also been able to connect with other businesses that want to sponsor our races and community events. There's hard numbers associated with that. I'm projecting that this year, we'll have two of our races completely sponsored, and over half of them sponsored in 2014.

"Heroes in Recovery has now become a top-10 site for us— essentially over the course of a year and a few months. That is incredible growth from an SEO perspective. The stories that people submit … we can't write those kinds of quality articles as marketers. I can't pay people to write those compelling stories."

Because Lee's background is in the IT field, he feels especially connected to this growth. He continues excitedly, "It's interesting that our top three referring sites to www.heroesinrecovery.com are Facebook, Twitter, and StumbleUpon. We are generating and growing numbers based on social media and word of mouth conversations, just as we designed it to be.

"Heroes definitely generates calls. It's a top-ten website as far as visitors go, but it's in the bottom quarter as far as phone calls. However, those calls are growing every month, which is amazing, because we're not even promoting FRN on the site. Only one page in the whole site has a phone number. This site was not created as a lead-generating site. The fact that we get calls *at all* is a side benefit.

"When someone calls to talk to a counselor after finding us on any type of search, our counselors are able to reference the stories they have read on the Heroes site and refer people to do more research. We have a place to keep people engaged and that has a value.

"We were lucky that we were very data and metric-driven from the beginning. We built this community with the question in mind: How are we going to pay for this? That was a critical part of our success. We have been able to justify shifting a lot of our traditional marketing dollars into this movement."

Lee stops for a moment to reflect. "I have to be honest; if we can get those 20 million to convert to the 3 [million already seeking help], that's the win. They may not do that on the Heroes site, and we are fine with that. We just want them to be inspired and search in their local area. We want them to go talk to their doctor, go talk to their pastor, go talk to someone. *That's* the real win."

"I feel sorry for anyone who isn't sober."

Those words recently came out of the mouth of a beautiful, 21-year-old woman who is taking charge of her own recovery. If you spend any amount of time with the group from FRN— many of who are in recovery themselves—and the Heroes lead advocates, you quickly understand how heartfelt a statement that really is. Recovery is not a sad or somber way to live. It can be and *is* joyful, and often both funny and fun. That is a story that must be told if we are to reach "the other 20 million" and their family members. The other side of addiction is full of hope, peace, power, and freedom—freedom from stigma, from shame, and from silence.

"We are a leader when it comes to education and a leader in research," says Lee. "We can be a leader in breaking the stigma."

FROM STEVE KNOX

Former CEO of Tremor (Procter & Gamble's advocacy marketing business) and Current Senior Advisor to the Boston Consulting Group (BCG)

"FRN demonstrates how establishing a culture of customer centricity is a strategic business decision, not a marketing tactic. This customer-first approach is a way of operating that will meaningfully differentiate you from your competition. Placing the customer at the center means you care about them. You wake up in the morning to serve them. You want to hear from them—in good times and bad. They guide you in your business decisions.

"Reorienting your organization's culture around consumers is hard work. It requires leadership at the top to relentlessly demonstrate customer-first actions. Every strategic business conversation from the boardroom to the backroom must start by asking the question, "What is the customer telling us?" Former Procter & Gamble CEO A.G. Lafley knew who his boss was: the consumer. He ran an $80 billion-plus business, yet he personally found time to visit with consumers in their homes to engage and talk with them. He demonstrated leadership actions to change a huge organization's culture. And if the man who ran one of the world's largest companies can do this, just imagine how much impact you can have at your company.

"FRN also demonstrates to us the power of social movements. People desire to be part of a tribe, something larger than themselves. We humans are hard-wired to behave this way. It's easy to tap into this tendency: Simply identify the social movement where your brand is relevant, and ride the wave. Social movements come in all flavors. Some are heroic as FRN. Some are fun, as we see with Red Bull's connection to extreme sports. And some are aspirational, such as Pampers's devotion to raising healthy babies. However, they

all engage the consumer on a different level than simply offer-ing a brand's basic benefits. Your work is to identify the social movement where your brand can play. And once you've iden-tified it, get involved. Build relationships and actively par-ticipate—not necessarily lead, but participate. Trust me, the benefits will amaze you."

FROM ED KELLER

CEO of word of mouth research firm Keller Fay Group and co-author of *The Face-to-Face Book*

"A successful word of mouth marketing strategy starts with the brand's story and is brought to life through tapping into a group of talkers by using appropriate communication chan-nels. FRN follows this process expertly. The story of bringing addiction out of secrecy and into the open is worthy of spark-ing and sustaining a conversation. The recovery community shares a common unbreakable bond that is strengthened through conversation. As referenced earlier from academic research, emotional discussions are best suited to take place face-to-face. The palm cards and other marketing materials designed to be shared face-to-face work as effective commu-nication tools to increase word of mouth for FRN.

"Being clever always makes for an interesting story. FRN went against conventional practice by organizing 6K races and not 5K races. That simple, clever act causes people to ask questions that result in a word of mouth conversation.

"It's interesting that many of the FRN conversations mentioned in the case study are with a small circle of people. As a word of mouth researcher and practitioner, I'm always struck by how the cumulative impact of private conversations between two or three people at a time can collectively scale to something quite sizeable and 'impactful.'"

PASSION
EXPLORATION
#1

THE Passion HUDDLE

Uncovering the passions within your team.

xoxo

UNCOVERING THE PASSIONS WITHIN YOUR TEAM

Ask employees to bring one thing from their office or home to your next team meeting. It should be a personal artifact that they will use to share a story about something they get enthusiastic about; something that energizes their soul, something they can't seem to get enough of. We've had people bring stuffed dogs, their running shoes, or photos of their kids. Ask them to tell you why they brought their artifact, how they demonstrate that enthusiasm and what being able to share it means to them. You'll also want to hear if and how their work with your organization nurtures this passion.

ASK THE FOLLOWING QUESTIONS TO HELP SPARK A MEANINGFUL DISCUSSION

What do we know about our customers' passions?

How do we help to collect and display, then amplify and celebrate their passions?

How can we make it easier for them to share their stories?

What do we do to let others know what our organization (and our people) care most about?

How could we become best friends and kindred spirits with our customers?

DEAR _____ , YOU ARE MY HERO

Collect love letters that your customers and advocates have sent you and put them in a shoebox. Set up a regular time (once a month or twice a year, for example) to gather a group of senior and junior employees in a room together. Have each person read one of the love letters out loud.

ASK THE FOLLOWING QUESTIONS TO HELP SPARK A MEANINGFUL DISCUSSION

How should we respond to this letter to let this customer know how much it means to us? (Be creative!)

What is the most important thing these customers should know about us?

What do we admire most about customers like this?

Who will take responsibility for loving them back?

What might happen if we treated all our customers like we will treat these—even the ones who haven't sent letters?

What product or service innovations does this letter inspire us to consider?

Love letters are a tremendous opportunity to engage these hand raisers. What's our plan to reply to let them know we appreciate their feedback?

WHAT'S OUR CAUSE?

Gather a large group of employees together and split them into smaller groups of five people. Find markers, index cards, and large poster paper. Take everyone offsite if possible; outside is ideal. (Fresh air always does you some good!) Have each small group work together to draw a picture of your brand as a superhero. Make sure they assign their superhero a superpower.

ASK THE FOLLOWING QUESTIONS TO HELP SPARK A MEANINGFUL DISCUSSION

What wrongs does our superhero right? (What's our hero's cause?)

Who does she/he protect?

Why do people admire him/her?

Who are the arch villains?

What is our hero's kryptonite? (What can render him or her powerless?)

How might this cause stand alone from our brand? (How is it about far more than just us?)

What are some stories that tell us that this fight is something people care a lot about?

How might we invite people to join our superhero's fight?

CHAPTER FOUR

Imagine you're sitting on your couch, working toward the bottom of a bag of potato chips when a fitness center ad comes on the TV. Quick edits and high-contrast photography show beautiful twenty-somethings with single-digit body-fat percentages pumping, pressing, pulling, and preening. Their abs and pecs and delts are glistening with sweat and their gorgeous faces are rapt with motivation and energy. The ad undoubtedly finishes with a web address and phone number and some sort of call-to-action discount. Maybe you call, maybe you visit the URL, or maybe you just close the bag of chips (or finish it, out of spite).

But now imagine watching this ad while weighing nearly 500 pounds. It would be like witnessing the moon landing or seeing a Hubble telescope image—a beautiful sight, indeed, but something from another world. It's something that seems disconnected, far away, almost alien to you.

You'll never see Marcus Miller in a traditional gym advertisement. Even though he no longer weighs 500 pounds and has lost over 150 pounds in the last year, he still tips the scale at 350. The thought of six-pack abs and shredded biceps aren't what motivates Marcus; they're not even on his radar. "When you're almost 500 pounds, you have to celebrate the fact that you just made it *inside* a gym," says Marcus. "It's not even what you do when you're there; you have to break it down to smaller and smaller steps."

Marcus had no interest in joining a gym or even talking about fitness when he was putting on weight.

"I didn't want to talk about weight at all. To even have a conversation about it with my mom brought me to tears. When you're big—and I have been big all my life—you don't want to talk about weight. You want to hide it, so you downplay it. It's a pretty crappy place to be."

But even though he didn't talk about it, Marcus desperately wanted to lose weight. And while he knew exercise was a crucial part of the equation, the gym ads he saw on TV—of sculpted bodies happily working out with ease—were not relevant to him or his situation. As far as Marcus was concerned, gyms were just for "fit people who want to get fitter." And he knew his own goal was much more daunting: "I can't think about needing to lose 250 pounds. I have to get that huge number out of my head. Trying to conquer that number is like trying to jump a huge mountain. I just have to start walking and do this one little thing today and one more little thing tomorrow. Even if I can only do five minutes on a treadmill, those five minutes are as big to me as winning a marathon. I have to celebrate the little wins."

Marcus is not alone. Only 15 percent of Americans belong to a gym. And of the remaining 85 percent, only 60 percent are even willing to *consider going* to one. While they're open to the idea, no one is speaking their language. It seems most gym and fitness centers are only talking to the people who are *already* in shape.

To say the fitness industry conversation is broken is a bit of an understatement.

Chuck Runyon and Dave Mortensen speak Marcus's language. As founders of Anytime Fitness, one of the largest co-ed fitness franchises on the planet, they've seen firsthand that being overweight and out of shape is a "pretty crappy place to be."

We were a little bit skeptical when Anytime Fitness first reached out to Brains on Fire. After all, aren't most gyms like airlines, looking to sign up more people than they could accommodate in hopes some just won't show up?

Despite our *unwarranted* misgivings, a small group from Brains on Fire visited the Anytime Fitness headquarters in Hastings, Minnesota, to meet the team and take a tour of the building. It was a sunny Midwestern day and the place was teeming with happy smiling employees of all shapes and sizes. There was an air of aliveness and energy around every corner. It was a company of wonderfully real people.

And we immediately abandoned any skepticism we still carried upon reaching the second floor and spotting a simple unassuming sign declaring the company's vision statement.

So what is our vision?
To improve the self-esteem of the world.

Sometimes a company's vision is so long-winded and vague it's hard for even the statement's author to recite it. But it had taken just a few well-chosen words for Anytime Fitness to elegantly define the company's values, beliefs, and goals. They don't have a vision statement; they have a passion statement.

Working with companies that have a strong sense of higher purpose is important to all of us at Brains on Fire. We're big fans of passion statements like these, because passion statements get stuck in your heart, and that's where magic happens. Passion statements take a stand and trigger *emotions*. We're like most people; we long to be a part of something bigger than our own lives, and we take this into account when determining a good business fit. In fact, one of the first questions we ask companies who inquire about our services is "Why do you get up every morning?" We want to know what drives the leadership, how they got there, why they do what they do. We want to know their story and if they passionately lead with their values. We believe, as authors Rajendra Sisodia, David Wolfe, and Jagdish Sheth proved true in a long-term study that was published in their book *Firms of Endearment*, that companies that lead with their values out-perform the market 10 to 1. And those companies are the places where we should *all* want to do business.

There's no doubt in our minds that Chuck and Dave lead with their values. They felt so strongly about their mission to raise the world's self-esteem that they wrote a book titled *Working Out Sucks!* It's pretty impressive that the owners of a company that makes a living off people working out are still willing to say out loud what everyone thinks: that working out *does* suck. But there are a lot of things that suck more. Like being short of breath after walking up one flight of stairs, or not living long enough to meet your grandkids.

So we were in 100 percent.

We learned pretty quickly after talking to the Anytime Fitness team, the gym owners, their customers, and doing some industry research and listening to conversations online that the fitness conversation is fairly limited. Sure, there's a big loud party going on; but the conversation is emotionally charged and contextually shallow. And it had hit a wall. It had limited appeal, but was failing to reach beyond the population whose passion is fitness and exercise. Anytime Fitness was sitting on a *big* opportunity, and, armed with passion and purpose, it had a genuine chance to open the door to something much bigger.

We were completely on board with Anytime's goals. We, too, wanted to wake up every day and help raise the world's self esteem, so we immersed ourselves in crafting a word of mouth marketing strategy and laying out a plan forward. It was during this phase that the amazing email below hit the inboxes of Brains on Fire. It was from Amy Taylor, our storyteller and community shepherd. She wrote:

"This is an incredibly uncomfortable topic for me, but I feel I'd be remiss not to share my experience/perspective as we're searching for a way to empower AF. I have struggled with my weight (and body issues) my entire life. I have seen the statistics and data. I know I should be going to the gym. I know fitness is important—and yet I'm not following through. Why?

If we're trying to inspire people to better themselves—and make the gym part of that betterment—we have to BEGIN by being able to talk about the issue at hand. There are all kinds of conversations going on about health and fitness, but people are terrified to talk about reality. People are talking AROUND it, and it's doing us all a disservice. It's time to get honest.

People feel uncomfortable even using the word 'fat' in our culture. We've created an entire vernacular to avoid ever having to say it. Plus-size, voluptuous, curvy, stocky, husky ... the list goes on and on. Our team is trying to wrap our minds around inspiring a huge population of people who aren't going to the gym—and who are [failing to live] up to their potential, reach their goals, and care for themselves. The simple fact that nobody here has felt comfortable asking me to chime in on this from the perspective of someone **WHO IS ONE OF THOSE PEOPLE** (and I haven't felt comfortable sharing it) speaks volumes about this unspoken conversation.

Weight, body issues, health, [and] self-esteem are all deeply personal [issues]. The current 'accountability' conversation taking place out in the fitness world is isolating, even if it is reality. Yes. I am the only one who can take responsibility for my actions. Nobody can go to the gym for me. But when the existing conversation is just a matter of 'only you,' it makes you feel alone. It's a heavy burden to carry. And it puts people in a mental and emotional state of isolation that has the power to drive them further back into a closet of shame, guilt, and isolation. It certainly doesn't drive them to the gym.

Before you can face a challenge, you have to be able to embrace it. Before you can embrace it, you have to be able to identify and talk about it.

If we are looking for the hole in the conversation—and what is lacking—here it is: We have a huge opportunity to start a new conversation based on the honest conversation everyone else is too scared, polite, or politically correct to begin. We can shake it out and create a space where people can stop tap-dancing and shuffling around the reality of things, and be blunt, honest, and straightforward. As soon as that reality seal is broken, people are going to laugh, heave a sigh of relief, and finally have a space to have an honest conversation about their lives, challenges, struggles, triumphs, motivations—and clear the way to start taking action.

When I read *Working Out Sucks!*, I felt an instant bond with Anytime Fitness. It is the first time in my life I've heard "fitness" people speak in a language that makes sense to me. They felt like my kind of people.

I have friends at home who think I am crazy when I talk to them over the weekend and tell them I can't wait until Monday morning to get back to work. Why do I feel that way? **Because I like the way what I do here makes me feel. And I like the people I'm doing it with.** I feel like I do what I do here better than I would do it anywhere else because I am surrounded by people who inspire me. If I fail here, I not only let myself down, I let down the people I care about, too. If I succeed, we all succeed. And all of this keeps me not only coming back day after day, it also inspires me to be the best me.

I truly believe togetherness is the key. Going to the gym may not ever be my idea of a good time, but going there with—or to be with—people I care about changes everything. Even if the journey is ultimately personal, nobody wants to feel alone along the way.

I believe this is our opportunity."

We were humbled and stunned by Amy's wise words. As she so eloquently put it, Anytime Fitness has an opportunity to shift from an exclusive focus on physical fitness to a more holistic focus on *life* fitness. We could give people a voice as part of a new conversation that they could own. A conversation that would not be limited to reps, muscles, and treadmills, but a deeper conversation about the things fitness enables us to experience in our lives. By becoming an advocate for total life fitness, Anytime could get credit for equipping people with the tools, resources, and support that enable them to share their thoughts and do the things they want to do. Most of all, they could help give a voice to the masses of anti-gym rats to redefine fitness *on their own terms.*

And so the Fitness Rebellion was born.

A big part of building a community begins with declaring your manifesto. It's an important way to verbally take a stand.

THE FITNESS REBELLION MANIFESTO

I reject the notion that beauty, desirability, and worthiness are one size fits all. I think happy people are the healthiest people. It's not enough to just look good on the outside. I want to feel good on the inside, too.

I will give my one, precious body the respect it deserves. We've been together a long time, and we've got miles to go. When my body is strong, I am strong. When my body feels good, I feel good. Wherever I go, my body goes, too. When I take care of my body, it takes care of me.

I celebrate the little victories. From the first pair of running shoes I lace up, to the morning I didn't feel like waking up at 5 a.m. to go to the gym but did it anyway. These are my personal triumphs, and I think each one deserves a parade.

I believe sweat stains are a badge of honor and each of my muscles has a story to tell. I will stop seeing the gym as time wasted working out and start seeing it as time invested in working on me.

I will turn my inertia into my momentum.

I will do something with my mind, my body, and my life.

I want to improve the world, and I believe that begins by improving me—because when I feel my best, I can be my best. And when I am my best, anything is possible.

This is my commitment to me.

A manifesto written from the heart hits on an emotional level that's hard to explain. Chuck and Dave tell stories of the Fitness Rebellion manifesto bringing people to tears. It speaks to an audience that has felt ignored, by giving them a voice and the permission to take control of their lives. A manifesto makes the conversation *personal.*

IT WAS TIME TO CHANGE THE FITNESS CONVERSATION

In order to give the Fitness Rebellion momentum, we had to start by finding the right people to *lead* the conversation. We began by searching internally for Anytime Fitness owners and trainers who were excited for the opportunity to inspire others. We knew they were people who realize that raising the world's self-esteem begins in their club and their community, and that it happens one person (and one little win) at a time. We were looking for people who were ready to start a conversation that no one else was having in the fitness world.

Considering that we were looking amongst people who were passionate about fitness, we thought it would be pretty easy. It turns out that it was tough work.

We set up an online recruitment site and posted out the call for "Kickstarters" on the Anytime Fitness internal message board. The announcement came in the form of a personal video from Chuck and Dave. Most people who applied admitted to being a little unsure of what they were getting into.

We made the application process pretty detailed so that it would also function as a weeding-out process. Only 100 people or so took the time to go through the application and submit their story. Chuck and Dave were a little bummed that so few from their organization applied, but we weren't surprised. We could have made the application process quick and simple; but we weren't looking for people interested in quick and simple. We wanted 25 people who were willing to put some real skin in the game.

IT'S ABOUT PEOPLE, STUPID

That line is from our first book and we live it every day. And nowhere is it more important than during the interview process for community leaders. Having the right people leading the community is critical to its success, and we don't take the process lightly.

During one rainy afternoon while interviewing the culled down list of potential leads via Skype, we found ourselves waiting yet again for Josh Cox. Josh worked at an Anytime Fitness gym in Santa Rosa, California, and despite completing the online application he'd already missed two scheduled interviews. Cathy Harrison and Geno Church from Brains on Fire had all but written Josh off as a possible leader for the Fitness Rebellion. (*Side note:* Igniting community is not like a campaign. Things can change along the way. We changed the name of the leaders at some point from Kickstarters to Fitness Rebels. The key is to trust the journey and the things you learn every step of the way. Igniting community is an evolving process; there are no mistakes.)

When Josh finally did appear on the screen it didn't take us long before we knew he was exactly what we were hoping to discover.

Josh told us *why* he believed in the Fitness Rebellion, and that he was actually doing something similar already at the club he worked at in Santa Rosa. We knew we had magic in a bottle and magic in Josh. You see, you know you have struck gold when you find what you're trying to do is already bubbling up organically in your own organization.

TOGETHERNESS IS THE KEY

Josh's passion to be a part of the Fitness Rebellion came from a place of empathy. Before Josh was a fitness instructor, he was an overweight kid—a 5'3" high school freshman who weighed 265 pounds. He remembers being teased, bullied, and constantly in fear.

"Two weeks into my freshman year, I was walking home from school and a group of kids were hanging out near some bleachers at a park on my route. They grabbed me by my arms and threw me against the back of a set of bleachers. They duct taped my arms and legs together. Unable to defend myself, the boys proceeded to tear off my shirt and slap my belly back and forth saying things like, 'I've never seen a belly so big move so much!' and 'I bet you won't ignore us now, fat boy!' After they had tortured me about my 'man boobs,' the group lost interest in the crying kid they had taped to the bleachers and left. As soon as I got home, I was able to sneak to my room without seeing anyone. I pulled on a new shirt, throwing the tattered shirt in the trash. The next thing I did was head to the kitchen to ask my mom to sign me up for a gym membership.

"I live with that memory every single day. Sometimes it makes me feel weak and pitiful, while other times it makes me feel like the strongest man alive. If I can make something of myself after that experience, I know there isn't a thing on earth that I *can't* do.

"The hardest day of my life is also the fuel for my fire. I'm thankful for everything I have ever been through, because in the long run it was training for my role as a leader. I know rock bottom in every way. I also know what sunlight at the top of a mountain feels like.

"It feels amazing."

It's got to be on their own terms.

Josh was definitely the perfect person to lead a community. Now he and the other 24 Fitness Rebels are leading the charge to change the fitness conversation. In his role as a Fitness Rebel, Josh wears crazy colored shorts and carries a shovel around the gym urging people to "dig in as a group," and make a difference in their lives. He spends every single day building camaraderie and forming a tribe along the way. Josh's passion for the Fitness Rebellion comes from his heart and his memories of being a bullied, overweight kid—and his appreciation for what it took for him to come so far.

Like Josh, each Fitness Rebel has found a way to internalize and individualize the Rebellion in their clubs and communities. From boot camps to Rebel "No-Fun-Runs," each community has its own unique Fitness Rebellion Flavor.

There's power in noticing the little things.

During their training, the Fitness Rebel Community Leaders were asked to find and share tales of little victories in an effort to help them *notice and celebrate* their club members' personal milestones. By noticing the little wins, they were creating a new *functional* conversation. They would submit these accounts to the Fitness Rebellion community manager. We would give the stories a little love (by smoothing out grammar) and then post them on the Fitness Rebellion site along with a photo. Other times we would just listen and help bring them to life. We also made sure that we shared the stories across all social media channels.

To help celebrate these little victories, we armed the Rebels with something we called Kicking But cards. Kicking But cards are about kicking your excuses to the curb. We can all find excuses not to go to the gym. "I would go to the gym, *but* no time, no shoes, no _____." Their purpose was not to commemorate marathons completed or huge numbers of pounds lost, but to acknowledge the little wins, like the purchase of a first pair of running shoes or showing up to the gym early on a rainy Monday morning.

Noticing the little things is just what Brian Kleinschmidt, another Fitness Rebel, did when he smiled at a woman on the treadmill.

It was the first time he'd seen the woman working out with her hair pulled back, so he gave her a compliment about how nice she looked. "Thanks," she said smiling proudly. "It's the first time in 15 years I have felt good enough about myself to pull my hair back in a ponytail. I'm no longer trying to hide." This victory deserved some celebration, so Brian gave her a "Kicking But" card when she'd finished her workout and wrote a personal note about her ponytail milestone on the back.

That same woman has earned six Kicking But cards that she keeps in her car. Whenever she feels like skipping her workout, she flips down her visor where she keeps the cards in case of a motivational emergency. The Kicking But cards help her find the willpower to make it to the gym. And the cards don't lie; she's definitely kicking butt, losing ten dress sizes in the process.

MEET ANYA'S LITTLE WHITEBOARD

Fitness Rebel Anya Edgley-Turpin's gym right outside of Seattle in Gig Harbor could not be more different from Josh's club in Santa Rosa. Anya has struggled with how to bring a Fitness Rebellion to her quiet, slightly older community. One day she noticed a lady on a treadmill in *work* clothes, rather than *workout* clothes. Anya asked what was going on and the woman replied: "I totally forgot my gym clothes and I was heading this way when I realized it. I said to myself, you know what? I'm not going to let that be an excuse today. I am going to go work out in my clothes. I'm going to get on the treadmill." Anya gave the woman a Kicking But card and handed her a whiteboard where she had written, "I am a Fitness Rebel because I worked out even though I forgot my gym clothes." Anya had gotten the idea from another rebel named Tanya who was posting whiteboard "I'm a Fitness Rebel because …" photos from her club. So she took a quick photo and posted it on the Fitness Rebellion Facebook Page. Anya had found her club's Rebellious voice in that little whiteboard moment. To this day her club continues to share their little wins and whiteboard photos online. They've found other ways for club members to dodge these excuses. For instance, women who forget hair bands have no reason not to give it all they've got. The club has a little bowl of hair bands sitting in the women's changing room next to a sign that simply reads: "Please Take One." The tiniest bits of encouragement can go a long way.

There is tremendous power in noticing the little things.

You see, if you are ever going to have a passion conversation and build purposeful touch points in messaging, you've got to have empathy. And noticing the little things creates empathy.

WORKING WITH PEOPLE IS MESSY

It's hard work. And emotional conversations are especially messy. The Fitness Rebellion is currently in only 25 clubs and it needs a wider net to make a bigger impact on Anytime Fitness's entire franchise business, not to mention the world. Chuck Runyon is known for being direct (something we love about him), and he takes a long sigh as we reflect with him on the Fitness Rebellion's early months of existence. "You know," says Chuck, "the Fitness Rebellion is absolutely infused with compassion. This is not for every Anytime Fitness owner. It's about *passion*. You can't fake passion. If an owner or a trainer within each club doesn't identify with The Rebellion, it just won't happen in that club. The Fitness Rebellion is not just a sign you stick on the wall."

As marketers, we want to make things easy. It would be nice if igniting conversation and creating community and culture were as simple as putting a few signs on a wall. But humans are getting smarter every day in this connected world where there are more cell phones than people.

And so, businesses have to be brave to lead with their values, and they have to do it with honesty and integrity. People can smell a fake a mile away. And while the payoff is not always instant, it is *real*. We humans always to want to make things simpler and automatic. We yearn for programs and campaigns and systems and processes—and in many areas of life, step-by-step plans work well, but there's no single recipe for igniting a community and developing a culture. The Fitness Rebellion is not about traditional marketing with a roll-out plan and media schedule for each club to duplicate. It's personal, it's real, and it's evolving.

As we're writing these words, the Fitness Rebellion is slow going. There are signs of encouragement, but it's simply too soon to tell how it will play out. The website views are growing exponentially and engagement is incredibly high on social media sights like Facebook where the Fitness Rebellion often has a weekly 64 percent PTAT (that is, People Talking About This and not just "Liking" it) score or higher. But a more important question might be: How do you measure the number of people talking about the Rebellion face-to-face, which is where most conversations—especially emotionally charged ones—take place?

What is the ROI of changing one person's life? Is there a metric for empowering someone like Marcus Miller to take that first uncomfortable step inside a gym? And how do we measure the return on creating close engagement between your employees and customers?

"No one ever regrets feeling healthier," says Chuck. "If we can make people feel better about themselves, we can help ensure that they make better decisions. If the world were a healthier place, I just think it would be a happier place."

How do you even *begin* to measure that?

We are truth tellers at Brains on Fire. Like Chuck and Dave, we don't sugarcoat things. Obesity and low self-esteem are *big* problems with no simple solution. But can changing the conversation at a well-run gym franchise really begin to change the world? Time will tell if we are winning. What we know for sure is this: They have a heck of a better chance than many others out there because they are fueled with passion and empathy for their members. People like Marcus Miller, who found community at Anytime Fitness, are proud to finally have a voice in the fitness conversation.

FROM STEVE KNOX

Former CEO of Tremor (Procter & Gamble's advocacy marketing business) and current Senior Advisor to the Boston Consulting Group (BCG)

"The Fitness Rebellion case study dramatically illustrates the power of micro targeting; that is, recognizing the smaller targets inside of your wider target audience. Clearly identifying micro targeting is a necessary step for incredibly effective word of mouth.

"Most brands face the issue of having to purchase media to properly target these segmentations. The problem with this approach is that it homogenizes the target and ignores the real consumer. The fact is that all women aged 25 to 54 with average income levels are not the same.

"Micro targets are the key source of a company's future growth. Anytime Fitness did not ignore gym rats or dedicated athletes; however, they identified a key source of revenue growth: the non-user of gyms with specific lifestyle profile. This is how Anytime Fitness is going to win and grow in the crowded fitness-club sector. In the language of Procter & Gamble, this is called prime prospecting. It's the hard work of identifying the micro target you can best serve and that can be your growth engine. Once identified, you must passionately connect with the micro target. And there's no need to treat them the same as all of your consumers. They are special to you, and therefore deserve your special attention.

"Successful brands micro target within their consumer segments. Pampers, for instance, wants to serve all moms with diaper-age children; but they want to deeply engage with the mom who is passionate about her baby's healthy development.

Apple wants to sell you a computer, but they really want to engage in a deeper way with artists, creators, and educators.

"The marketing lesson Anytime Fitness teaches us is: Find your micro target and dedicate the resources necessary to win big with these valuable consumers."

FROM ED KELLER

CEO of word of mouth research firm Keller Fay Group and co-author of *The Face-to-Face Book*

"Our research at the Keller Fay Group tells us health/fitness/ nutrition is a subject matter people discuss frequently. Many of these are among people trying to find a way to establish a better health regimen for themselves. Anytime Fitness is smart to focus its strategy on changing the fitness conversation from workout fanatics to average people. The strategy of helping people feel good about their road to fitness makes the fitness conversation relatable and approachable.

"Experiences are the foundation to long-lasting word of mouth. Positive experiences with a brand or an organization drive the most credible conversations, and those conversations are more likely to lead others to action. The Fitness Rebellion zeroes in on the gym experience for the average gym goer. The Kicking But cards function as an experience enhancer and reinforce the feel good story of people getting into better shape.

"Another smart element to this case study is how Anytime Fitness taps into its gym members to tell the story. The engine behind the Fitness Rebellion is the stories gym members share, and those stories are made more credible coming from real gym members, not from the Anytime Fitness advertising department."

MIRROR, MIRROR ON THE WALL

Most of the time, our tendency is to jump right in and try to answer this hard question before any others: *What does our brand stand for?*

It's time to reverse this way of thinking—and one way to do that is by digging into other brands' and organizations' minds. Make 30 cards (using 8.5" × 11" paper is just fine) with printed logos of various brands—15 for-profit and 15 not-for-profits. Mix the cards up. Get 5–10 people together (bonus points for including your customers!). Reveal the cards to your group one logo at a time and begin a conversation.

ASK THE FOLLOWING QUESTIONS TO HELP SPARK A MEANINGFUL DISCUSSION

Why do you think the organization chose this logo?

What do you think it means?

What do they stand for?

What are the three most interesting brand identities?

What are the commonalities between them?

NOW, SHOW *YOUR* ORGANIZATION'S LOGO AND HAVE THE SAME DISCUSSION

Listen for the language and sentiment that people use when discussing your brand's identity.

Does our organization compare favorably with the three most interesting ones chosen?

Does our identity clearly amplify what we stand for?

If it doesn't, what needs to change?

WINSDAY CELEBRATION

The way many organizations are structured can make it difficult to know when we've won or succeeded. Winning celebrations are frequently limited to the really *big wins*, which often makes them few and far between. An important indicator of strengthening culture and passionate bonds between people in an organization is *what and how* we celebrate. Think about it: Do you know a single parent who ignores their child's learning to roll over, sit up, crawl, stand up, and even walk—and only celebrates when they learn to run and jump? Celebrating *little wins* can make a big difference in creating momentum for sustainable success.

ASK THE FOLLOWING QUESTIONS TO HELP SPARK A MEANINGFUL DISCUSSION

When was the last time you celebrated a little win—or a big win, for that matter?

How do you define a win for your team?

How do we celebrate what makes our customers wildly happy?

Do we celebrate anything that demonstrates what we stand for?

What can we celebrate with our customers?

NOW CREATE YOUR OWN WINSDAY

Go ahead and rename every Wednesday Winsday, a day where you gather your team and share your little wins. Buy a bell or a megaphone or get some ribbons. Make it loud and unexpected. Never miss a chance to celebrate a win, big or little.

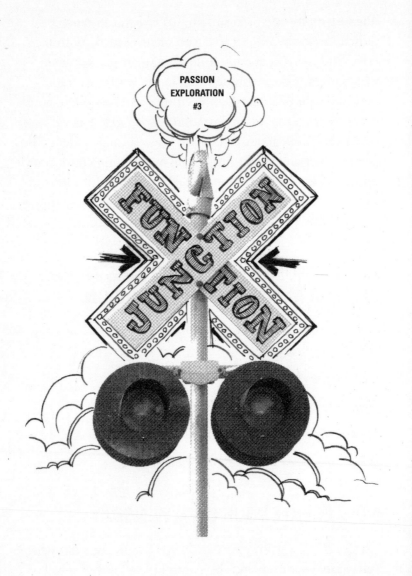

FUNCTION JUNCTION

Define one or two or three functional things your organization does. Do you build big buildings? Make scissors? Provide clean 24-hour gyms? Write these *functional* activities on a card.

Next, divide yourselves into groups of five or fewer. Then give each team permission to *play*. Find a park. Take a walk. Sit in the sunshine. Jump rope. The idea is to get everyone away from their day-to-day for at least 30 minutes.

WHILE THEY ARE OUT PLAYING

Have each group take the core function of your organization (for example, we build buildings or we make scissors) and flip it. Instead of saying "We build buildings" start with "Our buildings _____." Then fill in the blanks with a benefit that means something to your customers and employees. For example: "Our buildings build confidence." "Our scissors make memories."

WHEN YOU RETURN AND GATHER

Have each team present their findings. And ask, "What have we learned about *why* we are doing what we do?"

CHAPTER FIVE

Tamiera Harris sits in a middle school classroom in North Philadelphia handwriting an essay about her dream of getting a PhD. At the end of the paper she writes

> My dream is to let people know that they can achieve their goals no matter how many obstacles are placed in their path.

That was a big dream coming from a little girl who was raised in the Richard Allen projects in the early nineties, a 13-year-old girl who was sharing a small bedroom in her aunt's tiny apartment with her grandmother, three siblings, and a cousin. Drug dealers and gangs carrying guns and knives were right outside her door. Girls her age were getting pregnant in stairwells. Her daily life was filled with obstacles. She was always moving and changing schools. But from a really early age, Tamiera knew she wanted more.

Television and education were her way out of poverty.

ROLE MODELS AND ENCOURAGEMENT ARE POWER

Fast forward to 2013. When you talk with Tamiera the words focused, determined, and driven come to mind. And when she claims, "I keep my heels and my standards high," you know she means it.

"Growing up, I was inspired by shows like the Cosbys and HGTV," Tamiera says. "Bill and Claire Huxtable were successful and instilled family values. They stressed the importance of education. And HGTV showed me how everyday, hardworking people were going after the American dream of owning a home.

"My grandmother urged me to dream *big*. She encouraged me every step of the way. She's always been in my corner."

Tamiera had one other very important hero and role model in life: a teacher named Margie Goodwin-Washington. Tamiera's early love of learning and dreaming big did not go unnoticed by Ms. Goodwin-Washington, who approached Tamiera about applying for the Physician Scientist Training Program (PSTP), an extremely competitive program that streamlines a young student's education towards MD and PhD graduate degrees.

One of Tamiera's biggest concerns about the application process was not having the right clothes for the in-person interview. Tamiera remembers Ms. Goodwin-Washington saying, "Whatever we've got to do, we are *going to get you to that interview*. We are going to make it work." She took Tamiera shopping and helped her buy a professional black suit from New York & Co. for that life-changing interview. It was the very first time Tamiera had ever stepped foot in a shopping mall, and she remembers every second of the experience. "Having this almost-stranger just step in and really take an interest in me … was the most remarkable thing that has ever happened in my life," says Tamiera. And in the summer of 1998, "I was accepted as a trainee. Under PSTP, I completed research projects at Temple University, University of Chicago, University of Toronto, and Merck Research Laboratories."

Today, Tamiera is a Villanova University graduate, and has her MBA from DeVry University's Keller School of Management. She's currently a full-time clinical project manager and working on that dream of a PhD in health services at Minnesota's Walden University, all while making time to work on a book called *Projects to PhD*, her way to give back to the community where she was raised. She hopes to inspire others with a plan and a way out through education, setting goals, and simply by being a positive role model.

Tired yet?

Tamiera is also currently one of 10 hand-selected ambassadors for The DriVen Class, a community of encouragement that DeVry University and Keller Graduate School of Management supports. It's in that role that she is living her childhood dream "to let people know that they can achieve their goals no matter how many obstacles are placed in their path."

DeVry University was heading toward their 80th anniversary when they first approached us in 2010. They wanted us to help them build a sustainable word of mouth movement to encourage sharing and to celebrate DeVry and Keller students' success stories. And there were many, many amazing stories of success.

As a for-profit university, DeVry has traditionally been lumped in with the for-profit university media controversy that has been swirling about online and offline in recent years. That also made them the brunt of many late-night jokes: "How'd you get into to DeVry University? Um, I just walked in the door."

We started talking to corporate staff, teachers, students, and alumni, which is when we began to realize the *real* injustice of those jokes. Greg Cordell recalls with frustration in his voice, "Here we are, listening to story after story of people who are maybe working full time or part time and going back to school. They were doing it for themselves and for their families. They're people who want to make a difference in their lives, and who we should be encouraging and celebrating. Furthering your education is something we should applaud as a society. Doing that insight gave me a reason to fight. Call it passion, call it whatever you want; that's how I began to internalize the opportunity."

We also found out that DeVry is a really good investment. For the year ending with the October 2011 semester, in all DeVry programs and locations combined, 86 percent of graduates in the active job market were employed in their chosen field within *six months of graduation*. Students are employed in their field of study within six months of graduation. As one teacher put it, "I tell my students on their first day of class, welcome to the first day of your career."

We sat in on a few of those first-day classes and heard many inspiring stories. A lot of the stories were similar; most of the students had experienced some sort of learning break in life. Many had faced some sort of hardship: a lost job, a medical setback, or a financial hit, but they had one thing in common: They were determined to improve their lives and the lives of those around them.

Vicky Hammond was in on most of that early insight, and tells us, "The unifying passion beneath all of these conversations was that education was a gateway to a 'better *something*,' a better life for my family, my kids. Everyone we talked to had this internal drive to move forward. And education was the way to do it."

SOMETIMES A COMMUNITY NAMES ITSELF

We all want to feel a part of something bigger than our own lives. So we asked ourselves: How could we help the students and alumni and faculty come together to create that "*something* bigger" by helping them become *champions of themselves*? Could we create a powerful community of encouragement? The people we had discovered in our insight were determined, courageous, let-nothing-stand-in-their-way kind of people—but what else was there about them?

And then something came to us. When you look up the word "class" in the dictionary, you find these kinds of definitions:

- A number of people forming a group around shared attributes, a common bond, or shared goals.

- A group of people prepared for learning.

- A place for learning.

- Having qualities of exceptional merit; among the best.

- Elegance and dignity.

The people we had come to know and admire were in fact in a wonderful *class* of their very own. They were redefining growth, leadership, and education. It was evident to us they were already becoming a celebrated new breed of students and lifelong learners, a group of determined individuals: a DriVen Class. Together with the DeVry/Keller internal teams, we felt as if we had quietly unearthed the community name for this remarkable group of people. The DriVen Class began with a clear and simple mission to build a community of support and encouragement for people who were reaching for that *better something*. As Geno puts it, "This was a community built on helping people find a drive and push to move forward in their lives. It was oddly simple but pretty powerful and different at the same time."

WE WERE SEARCHING FOR LEADERS WHOSE PLATES ARE REALLY FULL

We placed posters at all of DeVry's 90 campuses, looking for people to lead The DriVen Class community. We sent emails and made campus visits to meet with students and staff face-to-face.

One of the things that struck Vicky as she went with the DeVry team on a monthlong tour of campuses in search of DriVen Class Ambassadors was that "The people we met on campus and who responded to our recruitment efforts are driven, of course; so they are busy. Their plates are *already* full. But yet they're passionate about giving back, and that was something they were all determined to find the time for."

In no time at all we had over 300 people apply to become ambassadors and help encourage other students to stay in school, face obstacles, and take care of themselves on the journey. We wanted people with different perspectives and experiences, who were willing to express themselves online (via blogs, Twitter, and Facebook). We wanted natural storytellers who were personable and willing to travel to attend local and national events. We wanted them to unite and become a force of positivity, support, and encouragement.

Justin Gillmar, the Director of Social Media for DeVry puts it well: "We live in a world where we are constantly beaten down in a lot of ways, whether it's your job, your personal life, your relationships, the media, or things that are going on in our society. There is a lot of negative stuff that goes on in our culture. To be able to create a positive and supportive space—a place you can go if you need a pick me up or just an encouraging word, where you can see motivational stories of someone overcoming an obstacle—is really a powerful thing. You see so little of it. If we can create that place with The DriVen Class, both online and offline, people will be drawn to each other and good things will happen."

We culled that list of 300 people down to 100, and then narrowed it again by interviewing the final 40 via Skype over a period of a week. Together with the DeVry/Keller team, we made forty 30-minute Skype calls that week. It was amazing to see these potential leaders in their homes telling their stories to us in person. Robbin recalls Chase Fritchle, the Senior Social Media Specialist for DeVry, turning to her at one point at the end of a long day and saying, "I will honestly never look at my job the same way again." When we asked Chase about that remark a couple of years later, he reflects, "Their stories were just amazing. It was hard to imagine some of the obstacles [these individuals had] overcome and see how that really drove them to continue their education and to push forward. Just seeing their passion and desire to really make a difference in others' lives, well ..." Chase stops for a moment and then simply says, "It just sat well with me."

As we sat in the front conference room of Brains on Fire that week, we felt as if each and every student that DeVry and Keller served had a remarkable story waiting to be told. Suddenly marketing a large university became very personal and very, very human. It became about Tamiera, Harold, Beth, Amber, and William, and all the other ambassadors. It became about real students with real stories. There was no going back.

IT'S THE RIGHT THING TO DO

Being a community leader or ambassador is a big job with a lot of responsibilities. While The DriVen Class Ambassadors were going to receive a small part-time salary for their commitment, the biggest reward of all was access to senior management and ultimately to each other. Greg Cordell explains, "It wasn't too difficult to differentiate between the people who were doing it for just some more money and the people who would have done it for no money at all. And you of course want the people who would have done it just because they believe it's the right thing to do." When you are looking for leaders, you are looking for people who believe what you believe so passionately they are willing to do it for reasons beyond money.

A QUICK WORD ABOUT COMPENSATION

We don't always compensate the leaders or ambassadors of a community. It's a strategic decision we make during the immersion phase. To pay or not is somewhat subjective and largely depends on things like the amount of travel required and weekly commitments we're asking leaders to make. One thing always remains constant; we are not paying people or encouraging them to endorse a brand—ever. We require full disclosure and follow the Word of Mouth Marketing Association's (WOMMA.org) ethics guidelines at all times. If we pay leaders, we are paying them to lead a conversation, to be honest and truthful, and most of all, to share their lives in hopes of helping others. You want to look for leaders who are willing to give up a weekend for you, who are so passionate about your cause they would be willing to help you without pay—even if you plan on paying them.

HOW DO WE CARRY THE TORCH FORWARD?

Igniting community and building strong bonds requires that we place people in an environment that allows remarkable experiences to unfold. We selected the U.S. Olympic Training Center in Colorado Springs as the site to make those very first remarkable experiences happen for The DriVen Class Ambassador training.

Laura Dagys, the Marketing Manager of Social Media for The DriVen class, says "I've been with The DriVen Class since it was born. It was crazy to see how quickly the ambassadors connected. In the span of a day, they became a family. Not a lot of people get to hang out at the Olympic Training Center and jump in the foam pit for gymnastics or play sitting volleyball and learn together how to overcome obstacles. Those shared special experiences connected The DriVen Class Ambassadors quickly, and also served as a very physical reminder of how much they had in common. Even though they were from all walks of life, they shared a certain drive within."

Geno recalls his experience at the three-day training sessions in Colorado and laughs, "We were all suffering from oxygen deprivation. This group came with a quest and thirst for learning. It was hard. We had long days. But we also had a lot of fun and it was very inspiring. The Ambassadors shared some very touching stories about where they had come from and where they are today."

"We play a lot of games where everyone, including us, has to participate and share personal stories. Everyone was just an open book," says Greg. It's important to find ways to get the leaders sharing beyond the surface. And games and play create an environment that breaks down walls. We become more kid-like, more ourselves when we are given permission to play."

The Ambassadors learned a lot about themselves and each other during that training. There was a powerful motivational speaker, a former special Olympic medalist, who shared his story. We also held sessions on the history and vision of DeVry/Keller. The ambassadors learned how to blog, be a trusted voice to others, and to connect on a personal level. We spent time talking about how to use the conversation tools and create events offline to encourage others to join The DriVen Class Community. The goal for training was to empower the ambassadors with knowledge so they could genuinely take shared ownership in building a strong and meaningful community.

They also made this promise to themselves and each other that weekend:

> I, _____, am a go-getter, not afraid to fail, a collaborator, optimistic, never-give-up, a believer, an achiever. I am a loud and proud representative of The DriVen Class, a community of encouragement, empowered by DeVry University, and its Keller Graduate School of Management. I offer my support, as a steward of this open forum. I will engage responsibly, reflecting the high standards we have set for ourselves. I will share inspiring resources, connect with others on their educational journey, and celebrate other ambassadors' success. I will champion our community's aspirations for career, education, and life. I will whole-heartedly support my fellow community members. Mine is the voice of The DriVen Class, the story of The DriVen Class, the promise of The DriVen Class. Together we will let nothing stand in our way.

A COMMUNITY HAS TO BE READY TO CONNECT AND EVOLVE

In addition to blogs from the ambassadors, the website thedrivenclass.com encourages students, alumni, and faculty to share their own inspiring stories. After a year and half, we've gathered some remarkable ones.

Most importantly, we've learned a lot. The website for The DriVen Class just underwent its first major upgrade based on what we've learned.

When you're dealing with a community, you can't be afraid to take risks. You have to be willing to adapt and ask: What have we learned? Community should shift and grow. DeVry has bi-monthly check-ins with all the ambassadors, and we're always adapting and adjusting. There's never a fear that we won't make the mark, because we know that if we fail in one respect, it's guiding us to make change for the better.

The new website allows visitors to create profiles and tell stories more easily. They are also able to share their college work online for others to see and have the opportunity to collect online badges for milestones and achievements. Additionally, class members have the ability to connect based on specific areas of study. It has been a great testament to never being afraid to keep the movement evolving. You are never done when it comes to community.

Chase shares with conviction, "Our students deserve to be put in the spotlight. We have some incredible students. We have some incredible faculty and staff. It's exciting to get those two talking, and sharing the things they are working on together."

SPEAKING OF CONNECTIONS …

Dave Messner is a determined 44-year-old DeVry student who does most of his course work online. He was two weeks away from graduating from DeVry and starting the Keller Graduate

School of Management when we talked to him about his experiences with The DriVen Class.

David explains, "I worked in the insurance business for 20 years before going back to school. I started part-time in October of 2010. One of the things that really piqued my interest about DeVry is the fact that you can get an online education, so I could do it on my own time and at my own pace.

He continues, "The DriVen Class has really given me the opportunity to meet a lot of people. I don't have a background in professional motivation or anything like that, but I do like helping people. The DriVen Class community is a great platform to not only get help from people in a cooperative, team-like setting, but also to help others. I visit the community a lot of times as a motivational tool for myself. If I have a quiz or a paper to write or even my midterms or finals in front of me, I sign into The DriVen Class and read a bit. It just seems to get me going."

When Tamiera talks about Dave Messner, you get the feeling she's talking about family: "Dave has such a bubbly personality," she says. The 29-year-old and the 44-year-old met online in The DriVen Class community and were connected by their determination to reach for, as Tamiera puts it, "something better."

One day when Tamiera and another ambassador were having a Meet and Greet on the DeVry King of Prussia campus in Pennsylvania, Dave surprised them both by driving 90 miles to meet with them in person. They put him to work right away. "Tamiera gave me a big hug," says Dave. "They wanted my help. It was just great! I met some great people that day and got to talk to them about my own experiences, which was fun to do. I really value the lead ambassadors and everyone in the community. Everyone's very professional and very uplifting. Their excitement just jumps out at you. Even if you're reading something online, it's almost as if you are right there with them."

SPARKING WORD OF MOUTH IN THE CLASSROOM

Dave's excitement is honestly hard to describe in words. He's worked really hard for his degree and frankly, he deserves to be excited—and *proud*.

"I sometimes wonder if I don't overdo it," says Dave. "For every course I've taken over the last year, I send an email to the entire class at some point during the semester telling them about The DriVen Class. I took an on-site class recently and my professor gave me a chance to stand up in class one night and talk about it."

Dave continues, "I asked if I could have some DriVen Class notecards to announce my graduation and they sent them right away. I want to recognize The DriVen Class as being a part of my milestone of finishing school."

A COMMUNITY IS ABOUT PEOPLE

It's not about Twitter or Facebook or blogs or social media. In fact, not one person we talked to mentioned the tools. When you dig into the real life stories of just two of the DriVen Class community members (and trust us there are many, many more), you get that message loud and clear.

From Justin at DeVry, "I guess what we do is marketing. It's also the people business. We're interacting with people all day, every day. You can't help but be affected by your interaction with people."

The DriVen Class has changed the way Justin and his entire team look at the work they are doing in the world. "What's my biggest lesson?" Justin says, "Don't be afraid to give the megaphone to somebody else. Don't be afraid to put the pen in your student/alumni/customer's hand and let them tell their version of your story. Relationships are so powerful." There is a huge lesson for all of us here coming from a very big organization. Don't be afraid to put the pen in your customers' hands and let them tell *their* version of *your* story.

From Laura, "It's something that goes a bit deeper than the day to day. We're clearly trying to get students in the door, push them forward, get them through their classes and get their degrees. But this encouragement is about more than getting through a class; it's about *life*, and finding success. Most of us don't have enough support and encouragement in our lives. Encouragement—that pushes us to do more and be more." The DriVen Class is doing just that by creating a positive conversation and supporting a place to find that much needed encouragement, even in really, really tough times.

It's a circle of encouragement.

After 22 years of work at an insurance company, Dave lost his job in November of 2011. Yet as a member of the DriVen community, it's easy for him to be optimistic about this experience: "Everybody was so encouraging to me during that difficult time. They actually helped me make the choice to go to school full time. The reason I've stuck with The DriVen Class is ..." Dave Messner stops mid-sentence to slow himself down. "It's kind of funny. I guess we both needed *each other*. The DriVen Class was just starting and I happened to be there to get the support that I needed personally to make it through a very, very troubled time. To tell you the truth, I don't know where I am headed, which is kind of scary, but really exciting. I think of it more as a positive than a negative. I can't imagine where I would be today without The DriVen Class."

HOW CAN YOU REALLY MEASURE THE ROI OF DAVE? OR TAMIERA? OR *ANYONE*?

It's hard not to smile when we hear Tamiera and Dave's stories — especially when we recall Justin's earlier words about The Driven Class:

> **"People will be drawn to each other**
> **and good things will happen."**

"It's not that The DriVen Class has to pay off in delivering this level of engagement or this many members, per se," says Justin. "It's more about the fact that we've only got a limited set of resources, and which bets *do* we make to drive our business. ROI for us is really about perception and reputation, and those things are very hard to measure. What is the value of raising the level of positive sentiment by 2 percent? What's the value of one really good story that 10,000 people see or hear—and that changes perceptions about our university? You can start to make up some metrics there, but it's impossible to really know. We have learned a ton in this last year, and I think The DriVen Class is going to be the most important thing we have as we move forward, at least from a social and community standpoint."

We asked Tamiera three more questions when we last spoke to her. The first two were: What makes you happiest these days? What makes you *smile*? She told us, "When I go back to my childhood and remember saying, I want to graduate from college, being able to check that off makes me happy. I want to be able to buy a house, being able to check that off. I want to get married— and I will be married next year. I like being able to carry myself in a way that people respect. I am living the life I imagined." And the third: So, what's your favorite set of words from a song? Her answer: "Don't ever give up on me …"

FROM STEVE KNOX

Former CEO of Tremor (Procter & Gamble's advocacy marketing business) and currently Senior Advisor to the Boston Consulting Group (BCG)

"The DriVen Class case study helps us clearly see the power (and impact) of community.

"For brands, this type of power is a combination of intensity and size. Big brands have an ingrained bias for size and scale. Every data point in their metrics dashboard follows the bigger-is-better mentality. This, of course, misses the impact that smaller, intense communities have as brand drivers.

"The secret to making smaller, intense communities work lies in effectively mapping social networks. As humans, we generally have multiple connections that move between numerous communities. By developing a deep understanding of how people make these connections, we can begin to see how brands can deliver intensity and scale.

"For example, a non-alcoholic beer brand learned there was a smaller but intense community of expectant mothers where their brand was relevant. The breakthrough came in understanding how this small community connected into larger social circles (from professional women's groups to moms' play groups). By building an intense relationship with the smaller community, the brand became a meaningful part of the conversation within much larger communities.

"This kind of social network mapping can only come about as the result of gaining deep consumer knowledge. And you only get to this opportunity if you are willing to engage in conversations with your consumer. Quantitative data is wonderful and powerful, but brilliant insight generally comes from mining the rich, unstructured discoveries that come from qualitative conversations.

"The new work for brands today is to understand where to find consumers' strength of community. Size and scale are great, but

you're far more likely to find real competitive advantage in small and intense conversations."

FROM ED KELLER

CEO of the word of mouth research firm Keller Fay Group and co-author of *The Face-to-Face Book*

"The DriVen Class reinforces that community is of the people, by the people, and for the people. Community is much more than people connecting through social media. At the Keller Fay Group, we believe that marketers should not be fixated on social media, but rather focused on "social consumers" who like to share their stories and hear other people's stories, and do so offline as well as online.

"Too many marketers strategize with a focus on the communication channels first and are instinctively driven to social media. What's my Facebook strategy? What's my Twitter strategy? What's my Foursquare strategy? (It's what's referred to earlier as check-the-box marketing.) Successful word of mouth marketing strategy must follow the roadmap of: (a) starting with a story, (b) tapping into your talkers, and (c) smartly choosing your communication channels.

"The DriVen Class starts with powerful stories of people gaining self-esteem and securing a better life through earning a degree. The word of mouth strategy is made stronger by tapping 10 ambassadors as talkers to lead conversations about school/life balance, day-to-day struggles, and affirmations. These conversations take place on a variety of communication channels from online social media to offline face-to-face settings.

"DeVry didn't start its word of mouth marketing strategy with the communication channels. It started instead with the stories to be told and the talkers who share the stories. More brands should follow that path to achieve word of mouth success."

WOULD YOU BE MISSED?

It's easy in the midst of our never-ending to-do work to forget about the value we add to others' lives. But that's the very reason we're in business in the first place. So take time to remind your employees about that.

GATHER A SMALL GROUP FOR 30 MINUTES, AND ANSWER THE FOLLOWING QUESTIONS

Who would miss us if our business ended today?

Would our customers be able to find another business that treats them as well as we do?

Would our employees be able to find another employer that respects them as much as your business does?

It might be nice to also do this same exercise with your customers, adapting the questions a bit.

Listen for and discuss the possible shared hidden passion conversations inside the answers to why customers and employees would miss your business.

If you happen to discover that your business wouldn't be missed, then you've got some serious matters to address!

PASSION
EXPLORATION
#2

SCHEMA BREAKER

BREAKING SCHEMAS

What's something routine that your company does and that your customers have come to expect—something they never challenge? Gather a group and make a game of it.

FIND IT AND BUST IT OPEN

Pretend you are working in an alternate universe, and list activities that are the somewhat opposite of what you are doing today, or activities that upend your expected services or products. Look for ways those ideas can help you break your schema.

Deliver stuff? What if you took stuff away? Or why not deliver happiness or jokes or _____?

Make shoes? What if you destroyed them? Or why not make footsteps?

Create marketing tools that connect people? What if you isolated people? Or why not be village matchmakers?

What if your customers worked for you? What would they do?

Make sure that, while you're exploring, you follow the ideas that are true to who you are. Of course don't throw anything out, but you'll be able to feel when an idea is different for its own sake and when an idea is different in a way that provides authentic insight and excitement.

How has this conversation helped you to think differently about the business you are in?

FIND THE FOUNDERS' STORY

Ask several teams of three to pair up and go in search of the story behind your company's roots. Have them present the story in their own way. See if you can get permission to interview the founder/founders if they're still alive. If not, figure out whether there is someone else they can interview, and where they can find artifacts. Empower teammates to tell the story of that journey and what they discovered visually by creating a book or video or music track—something more inventive than a PowerPoint deck. It can be as simple as sheets of 8.5" × 11" paper with cut-out photos, or as elaborate as an iMovie. The sky is the limit, as long as you keep the budget low (ideally, under five bucks). Capturing the founders' story can help to rekindle the passion employees have for your company, and serve as an emotional reminder to employees *why* the business exists and *who* it exists to serve.

THESE QUESTIONS MIGHT HELP THE TEAM GET STARTED

Why did our founder(s) start the company or organization?

Who was our company's first customer or donor?

What were our company's first days like?

What turning point led to our first success?

CHAPTER SIX

"Can you spell Wonderopolis?"

That's the question Josh Hallett, a dear friend of Brains on Fire, asked his 8-year-old son Trevor.

"W-O-N-D-E-R-O-P-O-L-I-S," Trevor says slowly and proudly, looking up at his Dad with a smile.

"Nice job, Trevor!" Josh says. He then turns and tells us, "By the way, you guys should talk to my mom about this assignment. She's about to retire after 30 years of running a literacy program with Johns Hopkins in Atlanta."

It was early summer 2010 and Brains on Fire, along with the team from the National Center for Family Literacy (NCFL), were knee-deep in the immersion and naming stage for a branding and word of mouth project for one of NCFL's latest educational programs.

NCFL is a major force in education and family learning based in Louisville, Kentucky. Since 1989, they've helped more than one million families make educational and economic progress by pioneering and continuously improving family literacy programs. Just spend a little bit of time with even one or two of those one million families, and you can feel the true impact of family learning. Parents who felt alone and scared—who felt that they lacked the basic skills to communicate and navigate the world—are now saying things like, "Anything is possible. Nothing is impossible. When you say you can do it, you can do it." Imagine the transformation they made, going from not even being able to fill out a simple school form for their children to believing anything is possible. Literacy matters, and NCFL is raising hopes and igniting dreams for families through the power of family learning.

When we first met NCFL, they, along with one of their long-term funders, had some new dreams and goals. They wanted to create an engaging interactive web-based educational tool to inspire families to learn together in a new and compelling way. They needed a name and an idea that inspired learning.

As NCFL Vice President Emily Kirkpatrick shares, "NCFL had both an incredible opportunity and a need to do something different and fresh for literacy. A very wise funder gave us permission to do something bold and . . . different. They didn't mince words. They let us know that this needed to be bigger and grander than anything out there in literacy today. With that came a tremendous amount of freedom, as well as responsibility."

NCFL operates according to a longstanding belief that family and community play an important role in learning. Study after study show that family, home, and community are the true drivers of a child's education. So the team at NCFL was intrigued with the idea of building a community support system. As Emily remembers, "We already understood that we should start by building an identity that could grow into a community of parents, children, and teachers who are using and enjoying our ideas."

After an in-depth knowledge-sharing meeting with Emily and her entire team in Louisville, we took off with NCFL to travel the country talking to parents about their kids. From New York to Ohio, we learned a lot about modern families. We discovered that many were really challenged economically and hard-pressed to find time to spend together. We learned there's no such thing as a typical family anymore; kids nowadays are being raised by single parents, grandparents, aunts, uncles, all struggling to find time. We also learned about resources for family learning, and learned that most are not free. We discovered that English is a second language for many families. The families we talked to all across America were stretched *and stressed*. They were trying to help with their children's homework, but most were left pulling out their hair after working all day in their own jobs.

"The idea of adding to a family's to-do list really won't get your very far. You've got to figure out how to add value to their lives and become a part of their routine if you really want to make a difference," Emily explains.

THE POWER OF SHOW-AND-TELL

We knew we were gathering valuable information; however, we still weren't sure how it could help NCFL define what they really needed to *do* in order to pioneer a new program that would make a huge impact. Where was the idea that would jumpstart this project? None of us were ready to cut off the insight spigot so we headed back up to Louisville. NCFL pulled together a series of working sessions with mom and dads. We asked parents to bring one learning tool they love to use with their children. It could be a book. It could be a toy. It could be a photo. They just had to bring *something*.

We conducted these working sessions with families of different ethnicities and economic situations to uncover common threads of family learning. These incredibly insightful show-and-tell sessions launched much deeper conversations. The visual cue that the physical items provided gave parents something personal to talk about. They weren't just answering questions; the objects they brought with them enabled them to tell a story. As Geno explains, "You have a greater chance of getting a talk-able nugget and a story when you ask people to bring a personal, visual reminder with them. It's going to be a very sanitized discussion when people are just answering questions. Focus groups seldom get at the real story."

LOVE IS A PARTNERSHIP

We fall in love with our customers as we catch their vision and gaze forward together. We love the word partner, and we hate the word vendor. Geez. So here's something to keep in mind if you're an organization who works with companies outside of your organization. Make your partners a seamless part of your internal team. Seriously, just blur those lines. Our relationship with NCFL and all of our ~~customers~~ (or partners, really) has been a wonderful, transparent open dialogue from day one. As partners, members of NCFL are willing to jump in, participate, and add their knowledge and expert point of view for every step of the process. We had many passion conversations along the way. It's funny to us that so many organizations want to hire an agency and say, "Do your creative thing and just solve my problem." They're looking for a magic bullet, but the world doesn't work like that. Real magic can only happen when people talk and collaborate and care passionately about the same things. We know it sounds so basic, but don't just hire outside experts—partner with them. We promise you'll always get more for your money.

IT'S NOT JUST ABOUT KIDS

The English-speaking adults told us during the insight sessions that they often feel lost when trying to figure out how to help their children with schoolwork. Kids in school today are learning things in a totally different way than their parents did. And because these teaching and learning methods are so changed, many parents felt out of the loop. Some turned to so-called "educational" websites to help their kids, but many worried these sites, full of games and questionable content, might not be educational at all. Plus, the education websites were just plain boring—at least for parents.

One mom said something that got stuck in our all of our hearts, *"You've got to inspire me as well as my child."* That was a big learning moment. A big *a-ha*! In order to inspire the children to learn, we have to inspire the adults.

On the flip side, we learned with Spanish-speaking groups that family was a major component in learning. They learn together as families far more than English-speaking families do, partly because they are often learning English together. They'll read storybooks together, face-to-face and even over the phone. A child might even call to read to a grandmother in Venezuela or Colombia.

We also heard loud and clear that the word *literacy* was lost in translation. When we said *literacy* most people assumed we were referring to the lowest common denominator, simply the ability to read and write. To complicate things further, some people completely misunderstood, thinking the word meant *illiteracy*. Redefining that term presented a big opportunity. NCFL had challenged themselves and us from day one to make the term much broader and more encompassing. Their hope was that literacy would come to mean learning in the everyday. It's about what we see around us. It's how we interact. It's how we comprehend. It's about how we interpret the world.

Geno recalls thinking, "The family that can't afford to go to Disney each year or visit museums all the time can still find wonder, amazement, and learning in their everyday lives. We could help them remember that."

Those insights were starting to shape some of our collective thinking.

We also began thinking about names for this new, inspired learning tool during this time. We had a list of interesting but still somewhat generic names. We were getting caught up in *edu-speak*, the jargon of the industry, so we knew we had to keep challenging ourselves to think outside traditional educational terms. The underlying question was: What is the *real* need for parents, and possibly teachers and children? And most importantly of all, how do we deliver the solution to them? From a strategic perspective, how do we get people to come back? How do we provide something to help mom and dad, grandpa and grandma, son and daughter, and teacher every single day? *What do we do?*

CREATING A THREE-LEGGED STOOL

Our insight told us that parents across all walks of life believe they are their child's best teacher, while teachers longed for even more parent/child learning to take place outside the classroom. But even though everyone agreed on that, there was a bit of a disconnect. "One thing that came through loud and clear to me during our insight was the passion and determination of parents to play a meaningful role in their children's education," Emily recalls. "But the parents and teachers were using very different language. They needed a way to relate to each other." NCFL had a big opportunity to build a wonderful three-legged stool between the child, parent, and teacher. That realization shifted our way of thinking from naming a program to naming a *state of mind*, a state of imagination, a place. It made us all wonder, "How can we inspire parents, children, and teachers every single day?" We began to make the leap from creating an identity for a program to creating an identity and a place that delivered wonder and curiosity in an awe-inspiring and talk-able way.

The conversations continued between NCFL and Brains on Fire. We even took Josh's advice and called his mom, who was set to retire after 30 years in education. She told us this story in her last week of work in the literacy program at Johns Hopkins. She was working with a lady who looked at her and said, "I just wish someone had told me to read to my child," Josh's mom recalled. "My heart just dropped. I had been doing this for 30 years, and I felt like I was back to day one. We all have to remember that this is a cycle. The scary truth—as it is with a lot of challenges we face, from obesity to addiction to literacy—is that people will always be *coming into* the circle of needing help." After talking to Josh's mom, we knew we had to build a place where it would always be easy to step into this circle.

Geno laughs and shares, "You know, you need to dig really deep to get to something remarkable. We wanted a name that would set up an expectation for both a child and an adult. We finally boiled it down to two names we had grown to love: One Million Eggs and Wonderopolis. NCFL loved them both because they seemed to set an expectation of unlimited possibility."

We all wanted something that could grow forever, largely based on the efforts of the people it was serving. The name Wonderopolis just kept rising to the top because it implied a location, an imaginary place to wonder. It also sounded new but familiar in an odd sort of way. It's a word that just sort of dances in your head.

GOING BEYOND A NAME

The next step, of course, was to figure out how to develop content for children and adults—and how to make it *interesting*. We started thinking, "Well, what if we strip it down to its essence?" We have a tendency today to make content so smart and thoughtful that it can tend to get, well . . . boring. An idea began to emerge. What if NCFL began to think of creating content at its most primitive and pure state? What if they did one thing, every day, and did it *really, really well?*

That's where the idea of the "Wonder of the Day®" began. And once we had that thought, the naming decision was easy. NCFL took the brave leap to bring this place called Wonderopolis to life.

ON OCTOBER 4, 2010, WONDEROPOLIS WAS BORN

The very first Wonder both asked and answered the question, "Why are flamingos pink?" The goal from the start was to make the wonders magical and enjoyable for kids *and* adults. We used words, visuals, and videos to create magic. NCFL was able to curate most of the content from the Internet. And, of course, that content had to fit the literacy needs and criteria that you would expect from a platform that NCFL created and led.

READY TO WONDER

In order to develop the Wonders, we sat down with NCFL and simply started wondering out loud about the things around us. We started looking at the ordinary visual things that had become so familiar to us *as adults* that we had forgotten to question them. If you begin to think about it, you realize that visual cues (and *wonders*) are all around us. A school bus drives by: Why are school buses yellow? It was nearing Christmas: Why do candy canes have stripes? Someone had a pencil in their hands: What are erasers made of? These everyday questions became Wonders of the Day®.

The look of the site is simple, with the background image changing each week. Altering the site's appearance on a regular basis creates even more reason to come back each day, as the backgrounds create a visual environment for wonder. It's as simple and refreshing as changing the placemat at the dinner table; it keeps things interesting and fresh.

JUMPSTARTING EARLY INTEREST

In addition to traditional public relations, NCFL created something we called a Wonder Jar®. Colorful Wonder Jars® were sent to parent bloggers and key educators in hopes of sparking a conversation between parents and *their* children. Wonder Jars were filled with a variety of different items: magnifying glasses, stuffed pink flamingos, compasses, and magic wands. Each one was different, but they all had one thing in common: They connected back to a specific Wonder of the Day®. We asked them to take some time to wonder with their kids. And of course, they were encouraged to visit Wonderopolis to check out the wonders. To our delight, hundreds of editorial and blog postings came out of that early initiative. With an amazing number of unique visits to the site during the first month, Wonderopolis was on its way.

TRUSTING THE JOURNEY

NCFL made some decisions early on to build really strong relationships with people. We actually went searching for people *to follow* on Facebook and Twitter channels, people we believed would find Wonderopolis valuable and useful in their lives. As people started following us, we followed them back and thanked them, not robot-style, form-letter thank-you's either. We thanked each one of them *personally*.

Teachers began to find Wonderopolis as they looked for something to help kick off their children's day. The Wonderopolis site was gaining their attention. This early group of teachers who were determined to give their kids the best resources they could find was an amazing gift, because they sparked the initial word of mouth within their school networks. Wonderopolis turned out to be a dream come true for teachers. It served as the perfect vehicle for them to jumpstart learning and student engagement in a fun way each day, and they started sharing it with other teachers. As Emily from NCFL says, "We have seen teachers connect through Wonderopolis. Some have come to see us as their professional learning circle, sharing lesson plans and new ideas with each other."

Teachers began visiting Wonderopolis from their classrooms daily. Kids got so excited about what they had learned, they would bring the wonder home—and it spread even more from there. Parents began learning from their kids, and then they'd go to the site to check it out. It created this wonderful triangle, that three-legged stool we all dreamed of in the early immersion stage, from teacher to child to parent. Parents have written thank-you notes to teachers for bringing Wonderopolis into their homes. Families are talking at dinner tables and in their cars about the Wonder of the Day®.

COMMENTS ARE A GIFT

NCFL decided from the beginning to see each Twitter follower, Facebook fan, and blog post comment as a gift, and they showed their appreciation by responding to every single comment and tweet. We also broke that unspoken Twitter rule that you don't follow more people than follow you, because that felt like nonsense to us. This is relationship building, for goodness sake; there's no need to keep score.

Shannon Kohn has been a part of the Wonderopolis team since day one. She clearly remembers the excitement seeing a community begin to bubble when the site first launched: "The comments from the kids are amazing. You can feel their excitement as soon as you start reading them, as well as [comments from] their teachers and parents. Community is *always on*. You never know when something is going to happen, when something is going to hit, when an opportunity to help spread the word will pop up, or when somebody might need you that day. It's like taking care of a baby or a plant. Building a super-engaged community is hard work. I think some people have this misconception that it just happens easily and organically. "

GROWING THE COMMUNITY

After a year of wondering, teachers raised their hands more and more and talked about how they were using Wonderopolis in their schools. They started making and sharing their own videos, and writing blog posts on their personal sites. NCFL really came to know the teachers who shared Wonderopolis, which was growing their national network. One teacher even asked NCFL not to use YouTube videos to help illustrate the Wonders of the Day® because school systems were starting to block YouTube—so Wonderopolis switched to Vimeo. NCFL was having a conversation and engaging in dialogue. Most importantly, their users have given them a new way to *listen*. "We have to keep our ears open every single day for opportunities to learn from the people we serve," says Emily.

EVOLVING AND GROWING IN YEAR TWO

On Wonderopolis's first birthday, a first grade teacher sent NCFL a video of all of her students singing at the top of their lungs, "Happy Birthday, Wonderopolis!" Shortly after that inspiring video, NCFL decided it was time for phase two of Wonderopolis. They began a nationwide search for six teachers and their families who wanted to become designated Wonderopolis Lead Families and go on a yearlong adventure with us.

We interviewed the entire family during this search phase. We finally chose six very diverse families with children ranging in age from 2 to 20.

All of these new Lead Families were invited to come to Louisville, which is a fun town and, more importantly, NCFL's home. We held the gathering there because we knew it was important that the leads felt a real closeness to NCFL and the organization's dedicated work.

While in Louisville everyone learned to blow glass, went to the zoo, and rode horses. We also learned about the history of baseball. Just like Wonderopolis, we tried to find everyday wonders that would be fun for adults and kids. It was basically *Wonderopolis Live*.

We also sent each family team on different challenges to learn from each event. "It was almost like [the TV show] *Amazing Race*," Geno remembers. "Each team got a little package each morning to open up. There were questions and you had to find the answers. Then, we would exchange what we had learned when we got together at night. We wanted to show them how to wonder as a family and share that with others. It was a fun way of creating experiences to talk about and share so they could continue doing that with other families." Geno laughs. "We ate breakfast, lunch, and dinner as teams. You have to really love people if you are going to lead a community. You have to be willing to participate. I stayed with the Nichol family. We called ourselves the Wooden Nichols. Our task at the Louisville Slugger Museum was to find out about a certain bat. We actually got to hold Babe Ruth's bat, which gave us *a lot* to talk about at dinner. We talked about that experience and shared our lives. We taught the families to blog and shared the functional part of becoming a lead in the community; but more importantly we showed them the value of sharing their learning experiences with others."

"Over those three days, we witnessed these families take a deep breath, ask questions, and see the world in a completely different way," recalls Emily.

PEOPLE ARE THE MESSENGERS

In addition to being a visionary literacy initiative, Wonderopolis is a word of mouth movement at its purest. Teachers, kids, and parents have carried the message and excitement of Wonderopolis forward. Although *word of mouth* has become a marketing term these days, the truth is that *you can't force it*. People will only talk about you if they are inspired by their own passion. NCFL has received significant media attention thanks to Wonderopolis, like being named one of *Time* magazine's top 50 websites in 2011, but the word has been spread mostly by people. *People*, not marketing channels, are the messengers. Teachers tell other teachers, kids tell their parents, parents tell other parents.

Wonderopolis quickly became a very valuable and *functional* educational tool in the classroom. It became something teachers found so helpful they were excited and proud to tell other teachers about it. But most importantly, it made kids excited. Children got *emotional* about the site and were eager to share the Wonders of the Day® with others, including their parents.

Katie Scully is part of the Wonderopolis team. One of her favorite stories is about a teacher who was out of the classroom one day because her son was ill. She and her students commented regularly on the Wonderopolis site, and even though their teacher was out that day, the students told the substitute teacher when and how they use Wonderopolis in the classroom. The students posted get-well comments to the teacher and her son, which sparked other students in other classrooms to do the same. It was cool to see comments come in from across the country, wishing this teacher's son a speedy recovery. As Katie says, "Wonderopolis feels like a magic tree house for learning. And it has room for everyone. It has no parameters."

RESPONDING IS PART OF THE MAGIC

We talk *a lot* about the decision that NCFL made to personally answer all of the comments on Wonderopolis. This is an important decision to highlight because, as the community continues to grow, this becomes a bigger and bigger commitment for NCFL. But there is no denying the fact that it's part of the magic. It's magical to the students when they see the replies they get back from Wonderopolis, since they're learning as much from the comments as they are from the Wonder of the Day®. They are learning to have a conversation and building their own digital literacy. NCFL is the wizard behind the curtain, leading kids, parents, and teachers down the road of learning. The organization enjoys encouraging its community along the way, and being there for them when they reach out.

There are many lessons within Wonderopolis's story—not just for not-for-profits, but also for for-profit brands. NCFL is truly creating dialogue with teachers, parents, and children by responding to them through the site. It sounds so simple, but so many organizations forget *why* this matters.

As Steve Knox mentioned in Chapter 1, brands often have a hard time understanding the importance of responding to the people who want to have a conversation with them.

Steve is a leader in the word of mouth industry and he has a great way of expressing why we must all work hard at creating a dialogue with our customers. Steve also has a way of connecting with people that makes you feel as if you are the only person in the room. Really. It's a talent we study and admire, and it's one that marketers need to study and emulate. We asked Steve: "What is the one thing that really bothers you about CMOs and organizations these days? What are they missing? What are they glossing over?"

He quickly replied, "One word: relationship."

Steve continued, "Historically, two conversations have taken place: a business-to-consumer conversation, which we call advertising, and a business-to-business conversation. But the new world has unveiled two others: consumer-to-business, where the consumer is talking back to us, and consumer-to-consumer, which is what we call *social*." Steve also points out the unfortunate but crucial fact that "the consumer-to-business conversation is the one we are ill-prepared for. . . ."

He pointed out that many marketers of large corporations use the fact that they have 10 million customers as an excuse. They say it's not possible to have a relationship with 10 million people. But Steve strongly feels that you have to start somewhere, particularly, with customers you want to have a conversation with, and who want to talk with you. Then, you just have to be open to what evolves from there.

MOST MARKETERS ARE STILL LOOKING FOR VOLUME

It's hard to articulate the value of meaningful relationships to marketers who still measure success based strictly on numbers. While keeping track of metrics and growing the numbers of people you connect with is a piece of the puzzle, it's certainly not the entire picture. You have to go back to what a natural-born people person like Steve gets intuitively. You have to make each person you engage with—both online and offline—feel as if they are the most important person in the room. Make no mistake: The kids and teachers and parents who take the time to comment on the Wonderopolis site are the most important people in the room. They grow NCFL's reach and impact every single day. They are helping NCFL change lives. NCFL shows us that by listening to them, valuing those relationships, and, most of all, responding, you can create a meaningful dialogue with the people you serve.

VALUING RELATIONSHIPS LEADS TO NUMBERS AND MORE

As of this writing, the Wonderopolis numbers are in fact pretty remarkable. Here's something we love: A majority of the traffic to

Wonderopolis is from returning visitors. According to a survey that online small business resource website COSE Mindspring conducted, an average of 28 percent of traffic to websites is from returning visitors, while 72 percent comes from new visitors. Wonderopolis is way above average, and we believe the large number of returning visitors show that these people are making the site a part of their daily routine.

Not only are visitors to Wonderopolis coming back, they're also coming from everywhere. During 2012, visitors from every state engaged with Wonderopolis, and these weren't quick clicks through, either. The length of time users spend on the site is well above industry averages.

Most importantly, visitors are engaging with the Wonderopolis community. From 2011 to 2012 the total number of authentic comments to Wonderopolis grew exponentially.

APPRECIATING THE INTANGIBLES

Wonderopolis has given us all a gift: It's making a difference in inspiring kids to dig deeper into topics that might lead them to be scientists, astronauts, historians, and journalists. Who knows what it can really do! It's wide open. Our world is limitless when it comes to wonder.

WHY FINDING THE PASSION CONVERSATION INSIDE YOUR ORGANIZATION MATTERS

Simon Sinek is one of our heroes. (You remember earlier when we told you to read his book *Start with Why*? Well . . . we really mean it. Seriously. Do it.) Many of us were stunned at how simply Simon stated the reason for finding the passion conversation in his brilliant book's introduction:

Studies show that over 80 percent of Americans do not have their dream job. If more knew how to build organizations that inspire, we could live in a world where that statistic was the reverse—a world in which over 80 percent of people loved their jobs. People who love going to work are more productive and more creative. They go home happier and have happier families. They treat their colleagues and clients and customers better.

Simon was of course setting up his reasons for starting with *why*. But we have to ask this: *What if more of us were able to talk personally about and know the actual people we serve, like NCFL?*

The entire NCFL team shares stories when we meet to discuss new ideas every week. As we hear these tales of wonder from teachers, parents, and children, it fuels our imagination and brings us all closer to the people we serve. It connects us emotionally to the work we are all doing.

Emily shared a story about a young boy named Colin, whom she met while visiting a classroom recently. "Colin had long hair and dirty fingernails. You could tell he was not from the best of circumstances. Wonderopolis is used in his classroom every day. Colin began quizzing me on the Periodic Table, which I confess I know little about! Then he smiled proudly as he schooled *me* on what Wonderopolis was all about. He made a parallel to Thomas Edison's approach to discovering things and inventing things. We had a long and wonderful conversation as he reminded me that Edison had no idea he was inventing electricity or the lightbulb as he was performing his experiments. His passionate conversation reminded me that we really have no idea what Wonderopolis truly means to children like Colin and to parents and teachers."

That's part of what makes Wonderopolis so powerful. We have no idea of the true impact. The possibilities are simply and wonderfully . . . *unlimited.*

FROM STEVE KNOX

Former CEO of Tremor (Procter & Gamble's advocacy marketing business) and current Senior Advisor to the Boston Consulting Group (BCG)

NCFL's Wonderopolis program showcases the critical elements of building relationships. Of course, the first step is finding and identifying communities; but the critical next step is building and sustaining relationships.

For most brands, this is new work. Marketers have not learned this skill. As mentioned before in this book, businesses have a tendency to hold the consumer at arm's length, which is bad news for everyone. But, as we also stated earlier, the good news is that our experience as human beings has given us all the training we need to develop and sustain relationships. We just need to translate our human traits into marketing traits.

We know from cognitive psychological research that advocacy is a combination of relationship and disruption (see Chapter 2 for an explanation of disruptive schemas). The harder of the two for marketers is the relationship part.

We form relationships in two ways. The first way is through dialogue, a virtuous circle of interacting through listening and responding that causes more interaction, listening, and responding. Relationships grow through dialogue.

The second way we form relationships is through a process called reciprocal altruism. That's a fancy term to explain where people freely give to others with nothing expected in return. NCFL illustrates reciprocal altruism. NCFL gives the gift of stimulation, ideas, and wonder. In return the consumer gives NCFL their time, engagement, and trust.

Brands, especially big brands, have a trove of gifts to give their consumer. These are not physical gifts, but rather, powerful gifts of information and time.

The new work for brands of all sizes is to search within and look for those small nuggets of information or time-saving gifts that can be given to consumers. Give these gifts willingly and often. Expect nothing back. They are a gift. Amazingly, a brand will get much more back in terms of deeper engagement, stronger commitment, and greater trust with and for your brand.

FROM ED KELLER

CEO of the word of mouth research firm Keller Fay Group and co-author of *The Face-to-Face Book*

Keller Fay Group studies have consistently shown that word of mouth conversations disproportionately happen in offline conversation (face-to-face and voice-to-voice) versus online (social media, text, e-mail). Wonderopolis is an online channel, but its impact occurs offline. It not only sparks conversations between teachers and students, parents and their children, and parents and teachers, Wonderopolis also sparks interactions. Conversations and interactions flow from teachers to kids to parents through the communication strategy of exploring curiosity.

The truly interesting element for marketers to note is that teachers were not the primary targeted audience for Wonderopolis. This case study is a great reminder that sometimes your best talkers are not the ones marketers expect will do the talking. Word of mouth can't be scripted, but rather needs to evolve organically in the real world.

The National Center for Family Literacy understands delivering experiences is a foundational requirement of word of mouth marketing. Wonderopolis is an example of a powerful strategy built around sharing a great story, finding your talkers, and wisely choosing your communication channel.

JUST ONE THING

Gather a few people to form a small team, and imagine that you can do only *one thing* as a company for your customers—just one thing.

USE THE FOLLOWING QUESTIONS TO SPARK A GROUP DISCUSSION

What would our one thing be, and how could we do it really, really well?

What would make us remarkable at that one thing?

What would make it amazing and fun?

What would make it awe-inspiring?

THE PASSION WALL

Create a visual inspiration wall of things your team is passionate and not so passionate about. Choose a monthly theme for your team to post about things that inspire them and things that don't. Hold group discussions about what people have posted. At the end of the month have someone unexpected create a recap or short presentation on these items and ideas. You might be inspired about what it says about your team.

USE THE FOLLOWING QUESTIONS TO SPARK A GROUP DISCUSSION

How do the things we are passionate about help others?

How do the things we love fit into the work we do in the world?

LOVE BOMB YOUR CUSTOMERS

Gather a small team together. Give them the names and contact information for five customers/advocates. It could be an advocate you find online. It could be someone who wrote you a great love letter. Ask each person on your team to simply call or email, or even write a real letter to your customers/advocates to let them know how much you appreciate them. Urge your team to see those letters and online comments as gifts.

ASK THE FOLLOWING QUESTIONS TO HELP SPARK A MEANINGFUL DISCUSSION

How did this exercise make us feel?

Did we learn anything new about our customers?

Do you feel closer to our customers?

Imagine you are telling your team about this experience. How will you retell it?

How can you do this with your own teams?

How can we do this internally for our employees?

CHAPTER SEVEN

SUSTAINING ~~WORD OF MOUTH MARKETING~~ LOVE AND PASSION

One of our main goals in sharing these stories is to show you how you can take a more commonsense approach to really understanding the basics of word of mouth (WOM). In essence, figuring out why people talk will allow you to craft some fantastic strategies of your own that truly mirror who you are as an organization. We hope you are starting to think differently about the people you serve and the conversations they want to have with you. As much as you might want your customers to talk about your products' and services' features and benefits, they (*like most people!*) probably want to talk about *themselves,* and how your offerings fit into *their* lives. They want to talk about their passions—specifically, the ones they share with you.

One of our core messages in our last book, and one that remains front and center in the stories we have just shared is this:

It's not about technology; it's about people.

Marketers have long had a tendency to follow the leader, even if the leader is wrong. And then, of course, there's that check-the-box mentality that we shared earlier. Everyone is jumping on the social media train, often using a technology platform as the jumping-off point. But when you claim to need "more Twitter followers, more Facebook fans, a Pinterest strategy," you are, as

Ed Keller says, "starting at the wrong end of the telescope. You're looking in through the wrong direction. So you are not going to see all the opportunities."

WHAT GETS MEASURED GETS MANUFACTURED

We work in a world where what gets measured gets manufactured —we turn to things like Facebook likes, Twitter followers, and Amazon reviews. We search engine optimize ourselves into next Tuesday. These are all opportunities to see and engage in person-to-person conversations about brands, but marketers often view these, and countless others, simply as success measurements; yet each one can be manufactured. And once a marketer has deemed a result worthy of measuring, someone will devise a way to engineer that result.

Do you really want fake numbers telling you about your business?

ANOTHER THING MARKETERS GET WRONG

Marketers focus intently on getting more customers, often at the expense of communicating with their current customer base. If you focus on passionate users of your products and services, and give them a platform and tools to share their love, they can *and will* show new customers to your door. And they'll feel loved in the process.

Banks, the auto industry, and cable companies are famous for ignoring their current customers when looking for new ones, so let's pick on them for a moment. We've all seen a great deal for cable that was just for new customers. Why on earth do you flaunt the fact to your reliable current customers that they are paying more than the newbies? Ed told us a story about shopping for a car, with a brand to which he has been loyal for many, many years. The dialogue while he was shopping went something like this:

Sales Rep: "Have you heard about our Conquest Program?"

Ed: "No what's that?"

Sales Rep: "Well, we give incentives if you have never driven our car before."

Hmmm. It's obvious, right?

To get the people business right—to understand how passions connect us—you have to *think like people*. You have to ask: Is that how *we* would want to be treated? Is that how we'd treat a friend or someone we *love*?

You need to work on making the answer a resounding *yes*—every single time.

SOME GREAT PASSION-FUELED, PURPOSE-DRIVEN NUGGETS FROM KIP TINDELL OF THE CONTAINER STORE

Creating the Customer Dance

"Creating the 'customer dance' is really our objective. This interaction focuses on the experience customers have in the store—and everything that happens after they return home. People have to go home and live with what they've purchased for a long time, so we want them to do a little dance every time they open that closet door ... because [what we've provided is] perfect for them, and frankly, because they feel an emotional connection to it."

We Love Our Employees Day

The Container Store has declared Valentine's Day as National We Love Our Employees Day. They give employees gifts, special recognition, and encourage customers to leave employees love notes on the company blog. The company also painted a love note to employees in an odd but noticeable spot—the rooftop of their company headquarters.

Chairman and CEO Kip Tindell summed up the core belief that guides the employee-first culture at The Container Store by paraphrasing this oft-cited quote from Southwest Airlines co-founder Herb Kelleher: "You can build a much better company out of love, not fear."

—From a 2012 Presentation at an Austin
Business Journal *event*

———————————

We talked about falling in love in the introduction. The stories of Heroes in Recovery, the Fitness Rebellion, Wonderopolis, and The DriVen Class are full of passion, hope, and people falling in love. And as anyone who has experienced it knows—love is amazing. It's a circular transaction. *You give love, you get love.* It really works just like that. And that fact is a big piece of *why* finding and unearthing your passion conversation matters so much.

Robbin judged the Word of Mouth Marketing Association's (WOMMA's) WOMMY awards several years back. She remembers a submission from a Fortune 50 company that has done a great job of connecting people who use their technology products to people who make their products. There was a question about return on investment (ROI) that a company representative answered with one simple, bold, all capital-letter sentence:

COMPLETE AND POSITIVE CULTURAL CHANGE WITHIN OUR ORGANIZATION.

That was it. It's stunning, really—and it's the *huge* opportunity in front of all of us in business today. Geez, that thought makes us tingle. We can and should form close, best-friend-like relationships with those who love us and want to talk with us and advocate on our behalf. We have watched that "complete and positive cultural change" happen within the walls of Foundations Recovery Network (FRN), DeVry, the National Center for Family Literacy (NCFL) and Anytime Fitness.

Chuck Runyon, one of the founders of Anytime Fitness, calls it "return on *emotional investment*." Just go hang out in the Anytime Fitness corporate offices and see if you can feel the return they have on emotional investments like the Fitness Rebellion. The energy is electric. Employees are engaged and having fun.

DeVry's goal and the way they are measuring ROI for The DriVen Class is to focus first and foremost on the positivity, support, and goodness, the program generates.

Don't you love that?

By uniting around a mission to break the stigma associated with addiction and mental illness, FRN is connecting with others who feel the same and creating a safe place for "the other 20 million" to step in and seek help.

Wonderopolis is inspiring both adults and children to wonder again—and showing tired, overworked parents and teachers that learning with their kids can be fun and rewarding.

Perhaps the most classic example of supporting the passion conversation is the Fiskateers, an often-discussed and studied community of passionate scrap-bookers. We were proud to feature them in our last book, and honored to help develop the concept. Based in Finland, Fiskars is one of the oldest companies on the planet (they invented the plow). They make beautiful orange handled scissors; you most likely have used or even owned a pair at some point in your life. They are so well designed that they are featured in the Museum of Modern Art. Fiskars makes other crafting tools as well, and while people aren't likely to talk about these tools' features, they *will* talk about what they *do* with those products—scrapbooking and sharing memories of their lives with their friends and family. Seven years after the Fiskateers community began, they are still talking and sharing about the things they love to do with Fiskars tools. They have become a part of everything the company does, and it's completely changed the way Fiskars develops tools—and how they see the work they do in the world.

OPEN HEARTS CAN HAPPEN TO YOU

The same thing can happen at your organization. By opening their hearts and reframing the work *they* do in the world, your employees naturally become more engaged. They become more innovative when they have close and daily contact with the people who use their products, buy their services, or support their causes. They wake up every day with a sense of purpose—and trust us, that feels good. They begin to *think* differently. Honestly, our customers are downright *protective* of their customers. They think about how their decisions might make their customers *feel*. It's wonderful to see.

AND GUESS WHAT—YOU CAN DO IT, TOO

You can. It takes a while, but being human is not rocket science. You were born with the natural skills you need to do this job.

Zappos is a great example that we marketers love to talk about and study. It's a company that's been cited so often that you might even be sick of hearing about it, but bear with us. We're going to look into it for the role the passion conversation plays in their organization.

Zappos delivers shoes and clothing to people all over the world. By tapping into a very real and basic human emotion, they struck an emotional chord, and empowered an army of customer service reps to simply "Deliver Happiness." That's something many of us wish to do every day. It's at the core of being human. Think about it: We are born to deliver happiness, and want others to deliver it to us. Babies learn at a very early age that giving happiness leads to feeling happy. I'm sure you've seen a grown-up melt at a sweet baby's laughter. It's called bonding. So how brilliant of Zappos to unearth and empower a company and its customers with this simple shared passion! Delivering happiness creates the kind of remarkable and emotional experiences that we long to share with others.

The simple two word mantra "Delivering Happiness" also does something else that makes people talk about it: It disrupts our normal assumptions about "delivery." Usually, delivery is just that: getting a package from A to B. Zappos doesn't *make* anything themselves. So they took a boring process like delivering a package and added an emotion we all want more of—happiness—to it. And it continues to grow from there. The following comes from the Zappos website www.deliveringhappiness.com:

> After the 2010 success of Zappos, CEO Tony Hsieh's first book, *Delivering Happiness: A Path to Profits, Passion, and Purpose,* blasted to the top of bestseller lists with its blend of business advice, tales of worm farms, raves, multi-million dollar deals, and—above all—the belief

that happiness can be used as a model both in business, and in life. And WOW ... did people respond! From Seoul to Lithuania, Sacramento to Sao Paulo, we heard an outpour of positivity from people inspired to make a change—big or small—towards happiness. So much to the point we couldn't help but believe that happiness is on the tipping point of world domination.

We love hearing about this journey of a passion conversation. Not only did it grow a company; it ignited a conversation that is sparking a movement.

CAN EVERY ORGANIZATION FIND THE PASSION CONVERSATION?

People often ask us this question, and the answer is a resounding *yes!* And sometimes the key is to *under-think* it. Quit trying so hard to solve a marketing problem, and instead start thinking about inspiring awe and wonder (or even happiness) in the people you serve.

So let's say you're embracing all this talk about love and passion and are starting to believe that emotionally investing in your customers can lead to *advocacy*—the ultimate goal of WOM marketing, of sparking your passion conversation. You're convinced you're in the people business now. You want to make a positive and lasting impact on your organization's culture, and lead with your values to grow your business. You're committed to tackling the assignments we've shared. You are abandoning your hope that technology and social media are some kind of magic bullet. You will not buy more books titled *Solve All Your Business Problems Today by Pin-Tweeting Your Faceblog on Instagramblr*. You want to find your true *passion conversation*.

You want to help *and celebrate* the people you serve and the things that matter to them.

HERE'S SOMETHING YOU MUST BE WILLING TO HEAR

Sparking and supporting passion conversations is a long-term commitment. Love, when done right, is an enduring thing. Word of mouth marketing is not about running marketing or social media campaigns; it's a growing, evolving process. As we said earlier, smart companies like Whole Foods and Starbucks spark love and word of mouth like second nature. Technology, traditional advertising, and point of purchase might play a role. Email, blogs, or content strategies might have a place. You will certainly need ways to communicate with the people you love—*the people who love you.*

WANT TO KNOW A SECRET TO LONG-TERM SUCCESS?

We absolutely *love* when our clients tell us, "We're on to something. I'm not sure where this is going, but we are on to something powerful." At some point, they all heave a trusting sigh and have a certain *a-ha!* moment.

So, if you are accepting our claims about love and the passion conversation, then you are buying in to long-term strategy. We think it's important to also remember that you need to find *some short-term wins to celebrate* so you can keep justifying the long-term efforts.

We're realists. We do live in the real world, and we know that everyone is accountable for the dollars we spend to help grow businesses or causes. We have done this well sometimes, and could have done better others—and it is something we are constantly trying to improve. So ask yourself out loud and often: *What will our short-term wins be? How will we measure them?*

Like Lee Pepper from Heroes in Recovery (from Chapter 3) explains, "determine your answers to the questions before they are asked." When you go beyond traditional marketing measurements, there's no limit to the return you will find. For instance, will you decrease employee turnover or increase happiness within your company? Think of measuring things that go beyond sales and marketing.

If you are in a large corporation, you might want to find a way to build a community while staying slightly under the radar. Yes, we are actually saying that out loud and in print, because this is the truth:

Community needs time to gain momentum.

Fiskateers has been around for over seven years; when they started, Facebook wasn't a household word yet. It took way longer than a fiscal year to discover the full impact of the community.

If you are signing up for understanding, sparking, and sustaining love and passion, you are signing up for the long haul. And frankly, don't you *want* a sustainable business/marketing/people strategy that keeps *you* sustainable as well?

Don't *we all* want that?

WHAT DO YOU DO WHEN YOU'RE "ON TO SOMETHING POWERFUL"?

What do you do to keep close relationships with your customers—and between your employees and your customers—once you get that momentum flowing?

How do you sustain that love?

1. **Tend to it.** You pay attention to the little things; feed and fuel it every day. Communities need inspirational leadership, as well as someone to hold that inspirational leadership accountable in a loving way. Because community leaders are often not paid—at least, not in strict monetary terms—the reward is engagement. The reward is love. Sometimes we manage the community for our customers, maybe just for a while before turning it over to an internal team. Sometimes we make an internal hiring recommendation. We do what makes the most sense for each individual community, but someone has to be responsible for noticing and responding. You probably noticed that we call the Community Managers at Brains on Fire Community *Shepherds*. They aren't really managing; they're gently guiding and urging people to stay engaged. They become a seamless part of the community. We don't hire for social media skills, because that's something we can teach. *We hire for passion.* Since we're in the business of inspiring others, we ask a crucial question whenever we hire anyone to work at Brains on Fire: We ask them what they like to do with their spare time. We love seeing eyes light up as we learn how people paint dog portraits or arrange flowers or volunteer to read to children. People who *get* passionate can *inspire passion* in others.

2. **Focus on the early engagers.** They fell in love with you first. DeVry student Dave, who you met in Chapter 5, is the fifteenth person to join The DriVen Class. We adore him. He tells everyone that The DriVen Class is what gave him the will to continue on and get his

degree, even after losing his job. That's a win for DeVry, from a dollar and cents point of view, and a big win for Dave as well. Always remember: *Energy flows where energy goes.* You have to hold a lot of hands to get that early momentum. You have to notice every hand-raiser and every little *everything* they do and say. And you have to show them you truly appreciate it.

3. **Keep it exciting.** You must keep your advocates coming back. You might decide, as Wonderopolis did, to "just do one thing really, really well." Whatever it is you choose to do, keep it fun. Share stories often to keep your internal team engaged. Try new things. We love that FRN is open and excited to host surf competitions under the banner of Heroes in Recovery. They are more than willing to jump out and try new things that their community suggests.

4. **Go out on dates.** Get together face-to-face as often as you can, like Heroes does with their 6Ks. Running, or some form of exercise, is often a part of the recovery process. Heroes will show up. Where do *your* loyal customers already go? How can you show up at their parties? We loved hearing the story of Costa del Mar sunglasses, a company that targets most of its marketing efforts on serious fisherman. Over time, the company noticed its brand had become popular with the college fraternity crowd. Instead of blowing a good thing by marketing at these groups—and potentially making themselves un-cool—they started going around to frat parties bringing in some great live music acts and handing out free sunglasses as a way to say thank you. It's hard work to coordinate that effort, but showing that gratitude felt right.

5. **Show kindness, respect, and admiration.** *Always*. You must begin to see comments on a website or via social media as a gift. Do you surprise and delight people who go out of their way to advocate for you? Simple things go a long way to sustaining love and passion.

6. **Live and learn.** Be willing to zig and zag and change your mind. If you are getting traction somewhere unexpected, go there. Be adventurous. Goodness knows the people who love you have innovative and smart ideas that are easier to execute than you might imagine. Remember those whiteboards at the Anytime Fitness in Seattle? Or Sean's recovery road trip? The next great idea could be anywhere! Ask yourself, "What are we learning?" around every corner.

7. **Renew your vows to each other.** Call up some members of the community or your leaders and just *talk*. Maybe even record it and listen to it as a team. You will find amazing nuggets hidden (and sometimes not so hidden) in those conversations. Just like we found while conducting interviews for this book, you will uncover new stories. You will renew your energy. *You will grow.*

8. **Remember that you aren't in this alone.** No solitary person can accomplish a *passion conversation*, nor can a marketing agency, a brand, or even the consumer. It takes both the brand and the consumer to come together. The passion inside has to match the passion on the outside. If one person has this passion and the other person lacks it, the relationship is going to end sooner or later.

9. **Look for and appreciate diversity.** When we look for people to lead a community, we purposely seek out different kinds of people. Think of the 25 Fitness Rebels. Trust us—all of them were unique, as were The DriVen Class ambassadors. Diversity keeps the conversations rolling. It makes it easy for all kinds of people to step in and join you. Robbin tells the following story about a lesson she learned in college about how even people who seem to have very little in common can form a strong and lasting bond through shared passions.

In short: Strong communities embrace diversity.

From Robbin, a Big-Time Johnny Cash Fan

When I was about 19, I worked in a country western music bar in my small hometown. I loved and still love the storytelling aspect of country music.

The group that worked there was an eclectic mix. We cooked and waited on tables and served drinks until the doors closed at 2 a.m. I was in college and found myself working with a woman about my age who was also the mother of a 4-year-old and had a piano-player boyfriend. The cook was a 35-year-old man who had lived in his grandmother's spare room all of his life, and who wrote song lyrics when he couldn't sleep. The bartender was studying to be a chiropractor in New Zealand, his homeland, and was genuinely intrigued with the collection of bands that played on our stage. Every night after the doors closed, we would sit for about an hour while the world slept, and we would just talk about the night—the music, the people, the community that loved our small-time, eclectic group of traveling bands.

I loved that job and those people. *I loved hearing the mom's boyfriend play piano (which he had learned to play by ear) as we talked late at night. He didn't have his own instrument, so he only got to play there as we cleaned up or in the local mall's piano store. I loved hearing the cook shyly read us his latest lyrics. I loved the New Zealander's fresh-eyed take on our customers and music. Even then it felt like an experience I would carry with me forever, and it really has been. I learned something magical that summer—the simple notion that community will form naturally and organically when you share common experiences and passions. Even people who at first blush appear very different will develop incredibly strong bonds around shared interests.*

_____

From www.brainsonfire.com/blog/2012/12/03/we-need-community.

We hope you can feel our customers' and our own collective passion coming through in these pages, and we hope that even a little bit of those feelings are contagious. Life is better when you embrace loving your customers and employees, and supporting their passions. Life is better when your customers love you back. Life is better when you move from the marketing business to the business of inspiring people.

Geno recently told the Heroes in Recovery story to a marketing group in New York. Afterwards, someone in the audience of about 500 people came up with tears in his eyes and told Geno his remarkable 11-year story of recovery. They instantly connected through a shared *understanding*. We've all been touched by recovery. Robbin was traveling recently and sat next to woman in a restaurant while working at her laptop. When the woman asked about what she was working on, Robbin told her about the book and the stories in it. When she got to Heroes in Recovery, the lady was wide-eyed and almost startled—she had been in recovery for 25 years and ran the Heroes 6K race in Colorado the previous year! And with FRN looking to open more facilities and grow their business in the coming years, you can bet that touching encounters like these will become more and more common.

The DriVen Class is also getting some new energy and an updated new website. Their goal was to have a certain number of engaged new members in a month when it launched in early May. We're one week in as we write this, and we're halfway there already. Communities seem to *incubate* (a Geno term) for a while, then something just tips.

And those are the moments that fuel our fire!

That's when we know the work we are a part of is something that *matters*. It's when we know we are touching lives, and that's worth all the time and effort we and our customers put into it.

HERE'S ONE LAST MOMENT OF TRUTH TELLING

We've shared a lot of smart research that has been helpful to us. We hope it will help you, too. We shared our processes and stories, and our customers' accounts as well as our own.

But you have to know this:

The *last* thing we want you to think is that there's some "secret formula" for igniting and sustaining word of mouth marketing.

Just as there is no formula for sparking and sustaining passion and love, there is no formula for sparking and sustaining word of mouth. That's because human beings are so intricately involved. And human beings are all unique. Every tribe is different.

Marketers tend to want formulas, but there are no formulas now. You can learn lessons from others, like the ones we have shared here. However, you have to stay faithful to who you are, and that simply means that there are no easy answers—just inspiration.

When it comes to connecting humans through shared passions, you have to look to your own people, your own tribe—customers, employees, and advocates—for your own magical and unique inspiration. Passion is very, *very* personal. Organizations can create moments that remind us of our humanity and make us feel good about ourselves, but if you try to *copy* what someone else is doing, people *will* notice. They can spot a fake a mile away.

When we first began talking about *The Passion Conversation*, Greg joked and wondered aloud: What if we just have a bunch of blank pages and two sentences:

Do unto others as you'd like to have done unto you.

Now talk among yourselves.

If you're the kind of person who just skims business books and then looks at the last few sentences of the last chapter . . . maybe you just got lucky.

Bibliography

Alcoholics Anonymous. *Alcoholics Anonymous: The Story of How Thousands of Men and Women Have Recovered from Alcoholism.* 1939.

Ames, L. *New York Times,* August 2, 1998. www.brainsonfire.com/blog.

Church, Geno and John Moore. *"Wommology: Dumbing Down Smart Word of Mouth Research."* Presentation at the Word of Mouth Marketing Association (WOMMA), May of 2012.

COSE Mindspring study, January 2009, www.cosemindspring.com/Topics/Marketing/Search%20Engine%20Marketing/What%20is%20good%20percentage%20of%20new%20visitors%20to%20a%20website%20compared%20to%20returning%20visitors.aspx#ExternalURLName.

Dichter, Ernest. "How Word-of-Mouth Advertising Works." *Harvard Business Review* 44 (November/December 1966).

Dichter, Ernest. *The Psychology of Everyday Living.* New York: Barnes & Noble, 1947.

The Economist, December 17, 2011.

Ehrenberg Bass Institute for Marketing Science. "Facebook Fans: A Fan for Life?" University of South Australia, www.marketingscience.info/assets/documents/275/Facebook_fans_A_fan_for_life.pdf.

"Ernest Dichter Papers." Hagley Museum and Library, Accession 2407, 1, 4.

Experian Digital Marketer report, www.experian.com/marketing-services/register-2011-digital-marketer.html.

Harris Interactive report, www.harrisinteractive.com/NewsRoom/Harris Polls/tabid/447/mid/1508/articleId/403/ctl/ReadCustom%20Default/Default.aspx.

Hsieh, Tony. *Delivering Happiness: A Path to Profits, Passion, and Purpose.* New York: Hachette Book Group, 2010.

Katchuk, Pam. Blog post, December 26, 2012, www.heroesinrecovery .com.

Kawasaki, Guy. *Enchantment: The Art of Changing Hearts, Minds, and Actions.* New York: Portfolio, 2011.

Keller, Ed, and Brad Fay. *The Face-to-Face Book: Why Real Relationships Rule in a Digital Marketplace.* New York: Free Press, 2012.

Keller Fay Group study, www.kellerfay.com/insights/four-wom-statistics.

McKinsey & Co., www.mckinsey.com/insights/marketing_sales/a_new_ way_to_measure_word-of-mouth_marketing.

Peres, Renana, Ron Shachar, and Mitchell J. Lovett. "On Brands and Word of Mouth," Marketing Science Institute, October 2011. http://papers.ssrn.com/sol3/papers.cfm?abstract_id=1968602.

Phillips, Robbin, Greg Cordell, Geno Church, and Spike Jones. *Brains on Fire: Igniting Powerful, Sustainable, Word of Mouth Movements.* Hoboken, NJ: John Wiley & Sons, 2010.

Runyon, Chuck. *Working Out Sucks! (And Why It Doesn't Have To): The Only 21-Day Kick-Start Plan for Total Health and Fitness You'll Ever Need.* Boston: De Capo Press, 2012.

Sinek, Simon. *Start with Why: How Great Leaders Inspire Everyone to Take Action.* New York: Portfolio, 2011.

Sisodia, Rajendra, David Wolfe, and Jagdish Sheth. Long-term study. In *Firms of Endearment.* Upper Saddle River, NJ: Wharton School Publishing, 2007.

Strauss, Neil. *The Game: Penetrating the Secret Society of Pickup Artists.* New York: HarperCollins, 2005.

Tindell, Kip. "FACE-2-FACE with The Container Store CEO, Kip Tindell." Presentation at Austin Business Journal event, February 22, 2012.

Acknowledgments

OF ALL THE WORDS IN THIS BOOK,
THESE TWO MIGHT BE THE
MOST IMPORTANT

To all the extraordinary people who inspire the remarkable organizations featured in this book. You've won our hearts with your dreams, courage, and passion for making a real difference in the lives of so many people. We are deeply grateful for the opportunity to share your stories.

Thank you, Steve Knox and Ed Keller, for the countless times you let us interrupt your busy lives for your smart observations. Anytime we get the chance to be in your company, we'll take it!

Thank you, Sean Madden, Nathan Spainhour, Greg Ramsey along with the entire Brains on Fire team for contributing to the artwork inside our book's pages.

Thank you, Christine Moore, Tiffany Colon, Shannon Vargo, Deborah Schindlar, and the entire team at John Wiley & Sons.

Thanks also to Neil Batavia—because no one ever remembers to thank their lawyer.

And last, but not least, thank you to those passionate souls, who know what it means to be Brains on Fire. Thank you for believing that marketing *should* actually be good for people and for the *thoughtful, inspiring, powerful things* you do to prove it every single day: Thank you, Brandy Amidon, Kim Banks, Alexis Bass, Rachel Bass, Allie Blalock, Megan Byrd, Eric Dodds, Emily Everhart, Justine Foo, Justin Gammon, Jennifer Goff, Mike Goot, Jon Hammond, Vicky Hammond, Cathy Harrison, Dan Heath, Kim Hebert Fairchilds, Mary Susan Henderson, Jackie Huba, Liza Jones, Shannon Kohn, Sean Madden, Kate McCarthy, Moe Megan, Laura Morton, Jon Mueller, Alison Quarles, Greg Ramsey, Carol Reeves, Taryn Scher, Katie Scully, Peter Sims, Nathan Spainhour, Zach Suggs, Amy Taylor, Kate Thompson, Steven Tingle, Jack Welch, Eric Whitlock, Libby Williams, and Heather Winburn.

About the Authors

Brains on Fire

ROBBIN PHILLIPS

I'm known as the Courageous President of Brains on Fire. I believe happiness leads to success. I have an amazing life, full of goodness and sunshine and adventure. I work with some really smart people I call friends. I'm one of the co-authors of the book *Brains on Fire*. I love my two kids in a way words absolutely can't explain. I love the sound of children laughing—of anyone laughing, actually. I love hot yoga, cold beer, sunny days, and starry nights. I believe writing inspires thinking. I love to speak and share our customers' stories in hopes of inspiring others. I think out loud at www.brain sonfire.com/blog. I believe we all work better when we're having fun. I expect my business dealings to be profitable. I want to create positive change in the world. I believe love is a circular transaction. I try really hard to keep things simple. Some days I'm better at that than others. I am part of the Brains on Fire movement.

GREG CORDELL

I'm Chief Inspiration Officer at Brains on Fire, which means my job is to find inspiration where no one else is looking. I've never met anyone who didn't have ideas. The world is stuffed with them. New ones, tired ones, radical ones, clever ones, good and great ones. What we need are fresh, big, bold questions. Give someone an idea, and they will judge. Ask them a great question, and they will grow. This year I celebrate 20 years of being married to someone who, every day, teaches me more about love than I knew the day before. I try just to live up to that and be a good example for my two children, encouraging them to ask good questions. And with any luck, on a really good day, our cat will notice that I exist.

GENO CHURCH

My official title at Brains on Fire is Word of Mouth Inspiration Officer, but I consider myself more of a pathfinder for our clients and colleagues at Brains on Fire; and I've been down that path with Fiskars Brands, Best Buy, Colonial Williamsburg, the American Booksellers Association, Charleston Parks Conservancy, the U.S. Office of National Drug Control Policy, the National Center for Family Literacy, Love146, and Rage Against the Haze (South Carolina's youth-led anti-tobacco movement). I wouldn't be here without a ton of support and love from my family at home and the Brains on Fire family. I'm lucky to be an explorer in conversations. I like uncovering the DNA of sustainable word of mouth movements and building them from the ground up. I'm a blogger. I'm a talker—you can find me at places like the Word of Mouth Marketing Association, the Public Relations Society of America, the American Marketing Association, the NewComm Forum on research communications, and the Customer Management World Africa conference. On Saturdays you'll find me in the spin room at my gym and cruising in my Mini.

JOHN MOORE

I take my job seriously, myself lightly. My serious business side is shaped from being a longtime marketing manager with Starbucks and later as director of national marketing with Whole Foods. For many years I operated my own itty-bitty consultancy, the Brand Autopsy Marketing Practice. Today, I'm happily cooped up at Brains on Fire, where I help ensure that our clients achieve their desired growth, and help Brains on Fire develop learners and leaders within the tribe. Along the way, I've solo-authored a few business books: *Tribal Knowledge*, a business management book, and *Tough Love*, a business book masquerading as a screenplay. My business travels have taken me around the world speaking to marketers at conferences big and small. My lighthearted side involves beer and music. I treat beer like others treat wine (my beer cellar is proof of that). I'm also deep into funky jazz and jazzy funk. (Think Sly Stone, Gil Scott-Heron, Meters, and anything that is "on the one." Dig?)

Index

Activities, meeting people through, 8, 11
Ad campaigns, 8
Addiction, 71–88
  breaking stigma of, 72–74
  and community, 72–77
  and Heroes in Recovery program,
    76–87
  reaching people struggling with, 74–76
Adding value, 48
Admiration, showing, 191
Advertising, 164
Advocacy, 22, 168, 186
  definition, 43
  and disruptive schemas, 61
  how conversations become, 64–65
  tipping conversations to, 61–62
Alcoholics Anonymous, 80
Altruism, reciprocal, 168
Amazing Race (television program), 162
Amazon, 180
Ambassadors (The DriVen Class):
  selecting, 129–131
  training, 132–134
Amusement, 54
Anonymity, secrecy vs., 79–80
Anxiety, 54
Anytime Fitness, 2, 22, 100–105, 183.
    See also Fitness Rebellion
  fitness conversation at, 102–105
  and the fitness industry, 100–101
  vision of, 101
Apple, 115
Austin Business Journal, 182
Awareness, raising, 81–83

Belief, trust and, 28–29
Berger, Jonah, 57
The Big Book (Alcoholics' Anonymous), 80
Blogs, 64
Bonding, 8, 11, 185
Bon Secours St. Francis Health System, 9
Boston Consulting Group, 21, 88, 114, 140
Brains on Fire (company), 40, 67, 192
  and Anytime Fitness, 101–102, 108
  being customers' friends at, 32
  Community Shepherds at, 189
  and DeVry University, 131
  Fire Sessions at, 12
  and Foundations Recovery Network, 74, 76
  "like" at, 54
  Love146 story, 55, 57
  mission of, ix
  and National Center for Family Literacy,
    151, 156
  truth telling at, 113
Brains on Fire (Phillips, Cordell, Church, and
    Moore), ix–x, 1, 22
Brand, YOU as, 13–14
Brand drivers, 140
Broadcasting, online conversations and, 62
Business-to-business conversation, 164

"Called to Serve with _____" (prompt),
    9–10
The Canyon, 72
Cash, Johnny, 192
Catholic Health System, 9
Chanel, 32
Check-the-box marketing strategy, 42, 141, 179

Cheerios, 57
Chief Inspiration Officers, 26
Chief Love Officers, 3, 23, 27
Chilling and watching TV, 6–7
Chrysler, 24
Church, Geno, 34–35, 40, 50–51, 73, 108, 193
 Brains on Fire, ix–x, 1, 22
 on DriVen Class, 129, 133
 on show and tell, 153–154
 on Wonderopolis, 157, 162
Closeness, creating, 13
Coke, 57
Community:
 and addiction, 72–77
 connections and evolution in, 134–135
 development of, 188
 igniting movements in, 79
 impact of addiction on, 76
 people as focus of, 137–138
 process of igniting, 108
 role of, in learning, 152
 Wonderopolis, 160–161
Community engagement, 31–32
Community leaders:
 compensation of, 132
 selecting, 108
Community of encouragement, 128–129
Community support systems, 152
Compensation, for community leaders, 132
Connections:
 in The DriVen Class, 135–136
 in Heroes in Recovery program, 84–85
 in Wonderopolis, 159–160
Consideration, conversations leading to, 27–28
Consumers, social, 141
Consumer-to-business conversations, 164
Consumer-to-consumer conversations, 164
The Container Store, 181–182
Content driven websites, 75
Contentment, 54
Conversation(s), 89, 191. *See also specific types*
 and consideration, 27–28
 and how it becomes advocacy, 64–65
 motivating, 42–43
 offline, 169
 shared-passion, 65–67
 sparking, with visual cues, 57
 tipping, to advocacy with passion, 61–62

Conversation channels, 63–65
Conversation tools, 13, 57, 80
Cordell, Greg, ix–x, 1, 22, 48, 65, 127, 131
The Cosby Show (television program), 126
COSE Mindspring, 166
Cosmetics, 25–26
Costa del Mar sunglasses, 190
Cox, Josh, 108–110
Crispin Porter + Bogusky, 33
Culture, organizational, 88, 183–184
Customer(s):
 being realistic about your, 5–6
 centricity, culture of, 88–89
 connecting with, 66–67
 creating a dialogue with, 164–165
 emotional investment in, 186–187
 falling in love with, 154
 influence of advertisers vs. word of mouth on, 26–27
 lifetime, 65
 relationships with employees and, 4–5, 188–192
 treatment of existing, 180–182
"Customer dance," 181

Dagys, Laura, 133
Daily Huddles, 10
Data, poring over, 6–7
"Delivering Happiness," 185–186
Delivering Happiness (Hsieh), 185–186
Detractors (customer category), 66
DeVry University, 2, 22, 125–129, 183. *See also* The DriVen Class
 community of encouragement at, 128–129
 early engagers at, 189–190
 word of mouth movement, 126–127
Dialogues, relationships with customers and, 168
Dichter, Ernest, 23–26
Diet Coke, 60
Disruptive experiences, 59
Diversity, 192
Doyle, Emily, 34
The DriVen Class, 127, 129–141, 182, 183, 189–190, 192, 194
 connections within, 135–136
 growth of, 134–135
 Ed Keller on, 141
 Steve Knox on, 140–141
 measuring return on investment in, 139

and relationships, 137–138
rewards of leadership for, 131–132
selecting ambassadors for, 129–131
training ambassadors for, 132–134
word of mouth in, 137
Drug addiction, stigma of, 72–74. *See also*
Addiction
DuPont, 24

Early engagers, focusing on, 189–190
The Economist, 25
Edgley-Turpin, Anya, 111
Edison, Thomas, 167
"Educational" websites, 155
Eduspeak, 156
Ehrenberg Bass Institute for Marketing
Science, 32
Emotion(s), 101
and face-to-face conversations, 62–63
high-arousal, 54
low-arousal, 54
showing, 54
Emotional arousal, 54
Emotional conversations, 52–61, 74
and disrupting schemas, 59–61
face-to-face vs. online, 62–63
and Fitness Rebellion, 112–113
"like" in, 54
meaningful tools for, 57
and passion, 55–57
and showing emotions, 54
stories in, 58–59
and visual cues, 57, 58
Emotional investment:
in customers, 186–187
return on, 183
Empathy, 112
Employees:
aiding recovery of, 73–74
customers' relationships with, 4–5,
188–192
investing time in, 65–67
love for, 14, 182
special recognition of, 182
Employee engagement, 113, 184
Enchantment (Kawasaki), 65
Encouragement, 125–128, 138
Engagement:
community, 31–32

employee, 113, 184
student, 159
Exciting, keeping it, 190
Experian Digital Marketer, 28
Expertise, social, 50
Exxon, 24

Facebook, 31, 32, 42, 64, 86, 141, 160,
179–180
"Facebook Fans" (study), 32
The Face-to-Face Book (Keller), 89, 115, 141
Face-to-face conversations, 89
flowing and continuous nature of, 64
online vs., 62–63, 169
Face-to-face meetings, 190
Falling in love, 3, 14
Familiarity, 11–12
Family learning, 152, 153
Finding your cause, 68
Fire Sessions, 12
Firms of Endearment (Sisodia, Wolfe, and
Sheth), 102
Fiskars, 183–184
Fiskateers, 183, 188
Fitness conversation, 102–105, 107
Fitness industry, 100–101
Fitness Rebels, 108, 192
Fitness Rebellion, 105–114, 182
and emotional conversations, 112–113
and functional conversations, 110–111
individualization of, 109–110
Ed Keller on, 115
Steve Knox on, 114–115
and measuring success, 113
selecting community leaders for, 107
and sharing little wins, 111–112
togetherness and, 108–111
Fitness Rebellion Manifesto, 105–106
Fitness Rebel logo (Anytime Fitness), 51
Focus groups, 24
Ford, Betty, 73
Foresight, hindsight vs., 41
Foundational truth, 60
Foundations Recovery Network (FRN), 2, 22,
72–76, 183, 190, 194. *See also* Heroes in
Recovery program
breaking stigma of addiction at, 72–74
reaching people struggling with addiction
at, 74–76

INDEX

Foursquare, 141
Fritchle, Chase, 131
FRN, *see* Foundations Recovery Network
Functional complexity, 47
Functional conversations, 46–48
   face-to-face vs. online, 62–63
   and Fitness Rebellion, 110
Functional newness, 47

The Game (Strauss), 8
General Mills, 24, 33
Getting people to talk about themselves, 13–14
Gillmar, Justin, 130, 137–138
Goodwin-Washington, Margie, 126

Hallett, Josh, 151, 156
Hammond, Vicky, 128, 130
Harley-Davidson, 32, 51
Harris, Tamiera, 125–127, 136
Harris Interactive, 28
Harrison, Cathy, 108
Harvard Business Review, 24
Heath, Chip, 58
Heath, Dan, 58
Heroes in Recovery 6K races, 81–83
Heroesinrecovery.com, 71
Heroes in Recovery program, 72, 76–87, 182,
      188, 190, 193–194
   and addiction, 76–87
   advocate selection in, 79
   and anonymity vs. secrecy, 79–80
   connections in, 84–85
   history of, 76–77
   Journey Box in, 77–78
   Ed Keller on, 89
   Steve Knox on, 88–89
   measuring success of, 85–87
   raising awareness about, 81–83
HGTV, 126
High-arousal emotions, 54
Hindsight, foresight vs., 41
Hiring for passion, 189
Homer, 34
"How Word-of-Mouth Advertising Works"
      (Dichter), 24
Hsieh, Tony, 185–186

Identity marks, 76
Illiteracy, 155

Incubation, of communities, 194
Indescribable, being, 29–31
Individuality, 50
Information:
   providing customers with, 31–33
   sharing, 47–48
Insight, 41
Inspirational leadership, 189
Inspiring people to talk about your product, 39
Instagram, 63
Intangible benefits, at Wonderopolis, 166
Interest, jumpstarting, 158–159
Intimacy, creating, 13
Invisible, being, 29–31
Isolation, 104
Ivory Soap, 25

Jack Daniels, 32
Jesus Christ, 10
Johns Hopkins University, 151, 156
Journey Box, 77–78
Justice for Children International, 55

Katchuk, Pam, 71–73
Kawasaki, Guy, 65
Keeping it exciting, 190
Kelleher, Herb, 182
Keller, Ed, 29, 33, 67, 180
   on The DriVen Class, 141
   The Face-to-Face Book, 89, 115, 141
   on Fitness Rebellion, 115
   on Heroes in Recovery program, 89
   on Wonderopolis, 169
Keller Fay Group, 27–29, 89, 115, 141
Keller School of Management, 126–141
Kicking But cards, 110–111
Kickstarters, 107
Kimberly-Clark, 33
Kindness, showing, 191
Kirkpatrick, Emily, 152–153
Kitchen table passion, 35
Kleinschmidt, Brian, 110
Know-how, knowledge vs., 41
Knowing yourself, 4–5
Knowledge, know-how vs., 41
Knox, Steve, 21, 67
   on disruptive schemas, 59–61
   on The DriVen Class, 140–141
   on Fitness Rebellion, 114–115

on Heroes in Recovery program, 88–89
on Wonderopolis, 164–165
Kohn, Shannon, 160

Labels, 73
Lafley, A.G., 88
La Paloma, 72
Las Vegas, Nevada, 60
Leadership, 88
    inspirational, 189
    and movements/social change, 79
    rewards of, 131–132
Learning, 152, 153, 191
Learning in the everyday, 155
"Less is more" philosophy, 13
Lifetime customers, 65
"Like," in emotional conversations, 54
Listening, 65–67
Literacy, 155
The little things, noticing, 112
Live and learn, 191
Long-term success, 187–188
Louis Vuitton, 32
Love, 183
    for employees, 182
    falling in, 3, 14
    patient and kind nature of, 8
Love146 (organization), 55–59, 73
Lovett, Mitchell J., 50
Low-arousal emotions, 54

Mac, Bernie, 74
McKinsey & Company, 26–28
Mapping of social networks, 140
Marketers:
    common mistakes of, 179–181
    and deciding what gets talked about, 26–27
Marketing mindset, unlearning your, 19
Marketing problems, people problems vs., 20
Marketing research, 39–40
Marketing Science Institute, 42
Meetings, face-to-face, 190
Meeting people, 8, 11
Mental illness, stigma of, 72–74
Merck Research Laboratories, 126
Messner, Dave, 135–137
Michael's House, 72
Micro targeting, 114
Miller, Marcus, 99–100

MillerCoors, 33
MINI (automobile), 50
Miracle on the Hudson, 59–60
Momentum:
    sustaining, 188–192
    word of mouth-powered, 83
Moore, John, ix–x, 1, 22, 29, 40, 51
Morris, Rob, 55–58
Morrison, Sean, 83
Mortensen, Dave, 100, 113
    on Fitness Rebellion, 106–107
    Working Out Sucks!, 102, 104
Motivations, consumer, 24
Motivational research, 24
Motivations for conversations, 42–43
    emotional conversations, 52–61
    functional conversations, 45–48
    online vs. face-to-face conversations, 62–63
    social conversations, 49–51
Movements, leaders for, 79
Museum of Modern Art, 184
Music, background, in stores, 25

Nantz, Mark, 9, 10
National Center for Family Literacy
        (NCFL), 2, 22, 151–157, 183. *See also*
        Wonderopolis
    inspiring adults at, 154–156
    relationship between parent, child, and
        teacher at, 156–157
    show and tell at, 153–154
    word of mouth project for, 151–153
Net Promoter Score (NPS), 65–66
Newness, functional, 47
New York Times, 24
Nike, 32
NPS (Net Promoter Score), 65–66

Obama, Barack, 56
Offline conversations, 169
"On Brands and Word of Mouth" (Peres,
        Shachar, and Lovett), 42, 54
One Million Eggs, 157
Online conversations, 7
    face-to-face vs., 62–63, 169
    intermittent and sporadic nature of, 64

Pampers, 88, 114
Paramore, 57

Partnerships, with customers, 154
Passion, 1–2
 and advocacy, 22, 61–62
 contagious nature of, 3–4
 in emotional conversations, 55–57
 emotions as triggers of, 55
 finding shared, 65–67
 and functional conversations, 48
 hiring for, 189
 kitchen table, 35
 as reason people talk, 39, 42–43
 signaling, 50
 social, 50
 and social conversations, 51
Passion conversation, 166–167, 185–187, 191
Passion Explorations, 67
Passion statements, 101, 115
Passives (customer category), 66
Patagonia, 51
People:
 believing in, 28–29
 as focus of marketing, 20–21
 as focus of social media, 179–180
 listening to, 5
 making connections with, 7
 thinking like, 181
 uniting, through shared passions, 39
 what people talk about, 63, 65–67
 why people talk, 4, 40. *See also* Motivations
The people business, being in, 14, 19, 40
People opportunities, 21–23
People problems, marketing problems vs., 20
"People Talking About This" (PTAT)
 measurement, 32
Pepper, Lee, 72–87, 188
Perception, 139
Peres, Renana, 50
Periodic Table of WOMology, 44
Persistence, 11
Phillips, Robbin, 9, 48, 131, 183, 193–194
 Brains on Fire, ix–x, 1, 22
 on shared passion, 192–193
Phoenix Multisport, 82, 84–85
Physician Scientist Training Program (PSTP),
 126
Pinterest, 42, 179–180
Platforms, for customers' stories, 13
Positive experiences, 115
Positivity, 183

Procter & Gamble, 21, 24, 60, 88, 114, 140
Products:
 inspiring people to talk about, 39
 "souls" of, 25
Projects to PhD (Harris), 127
Promoters (customer category), 66
Promotional messages, 31–33
Proximity, 11–12
PSTP (Physician Scientist Training Program),
 126
The Psychology of Everyday Living (Dichter),
 25
PTAT ("People Talking About This")
 measurement, 32
Ptolemy, 34

Ramsey, Greg, 76–78, 81–82
Realistic, being, 5–6, 11
Reciprocal altruism, 168
Red Bull, 88
Reframing of marketing problems, 20
Relationships, 138
 and advocacy, 61–62
 as basis for world, 21
 building, 168
 of customers and employees, 4–5, 188–192
 The DriVen Class and, 137–138
 and knowing yourself, 4–5
 maintaining, 188–192
 meaningful, 31–32, 65–67
 online, 31–32
 social conversations in, 164–165
 at Wonderopolis, 165–166, 168
Reputation, 139
Research:
 marketing, 39–40
 motivational, 24
Respect, 191
Returning visitors, 166
Return on emotional investment, 183
Return on investment (ROI), 139, 182
Role models, 125–128
Runyon, Chuck, 100, 113
 on Fitness Rebellion, 106–107, 112
 on return on emotional investment, 183
 Working Out Sucks!, 102, 104

Sadness, 54
Schemas, disrupting, 59–61

Scully, Katie, 163
Search engine optimization, 180
Secrecy, anonymity vs., 79–80
Secrets, telling, 12–13
Shachar, Ron, 50
Shakespeare, William, 34
Shared-passion conversations, 65–67
Shared understanding, 193–194
Sharing, 2–3
Sharpie, 29
Sheth, Jagdish, 102
Short-term wins, 187–188
Show and tell, 153–154
Sinek, Simon, 5, 166–167
Sisodia, Rajendra, 102
Skype, 130
SlideShare, 40
Social change, 79
Social consumers, 141
Social conversations, 49–51, 62–63
Social expertise, 50
Social Fresh (conference), 73
Social media, 179–180
Social movements, 88–89
Social networks, 62, 140. *See also specific networks*
Social passion, 50
Social signaling, 50–51, 80
Social uniqueness, 50
"Soul" of product, 25
Southwest Airlines, 182
"Spider web" network, 75
Starbucks, 31, 51, 187
Starcom MediaVest, 33
Start with Why? (Sinek), 5, 166–167
Stern, Howard, 74
Stigma, of drug addiction and mental illness, 72–74
Stories, 58–59
Strauss, Neil, 8
Student engagement, 159
StumbleUpon, 86
Success:
    long-term, 187–188
    measuring, 85–87, 113, 180
Sweatman, Oliver, 34

Taking a stand, 11
Talking, 191

deciding what gets talked about, 26–27
getting people to talk about themselves, 13–14
inspiring people to talk about your product, 39
passion and why people talk, 39, 42–43
shaping what people talk about with conversation channel, 63–65
what people talk about, 63, 65–67
why people talk, 4, 40. *See also* Motivations for conversations
TalkTrack surveys, 33
Target, 6
Tarr, 84–85
Tattoos, 51
Taylor, Amy, 102–105
Technology, 7, 40, 179
Temple University, 126
Texting, 64
Theatrical productions, 29–30
Therapy, cosmetics as, 25–26
Tiffany & Co., 32
Time-distortion, 8, 11
Time magazine, 163
Tindell, Kip, 181–182
Title, ditching your, 19
Togetherness, 108–111
Tom's shoes, 51
Training, of ambassadors, 132–134
Tremor, 21, 88, 114, 140
Tribes, 88, 195
Trust:
    and belief, 28–29
    developing, 8, 13, 168, 169
    earning, 7
Trusting the journey, 159–160
Twitter, 31, 42, 64, 86, 141, 160, 179–180

Understanding, shared, 193–194
Uniqueness, signaling, 50
Universal McCann, 33
University of Chicago, 126
University of South Australia, 32
University of Toronto, 126
Unlearning your marketing mindset, 19
Ursa Major (brand), 34–35
US Airways, 59–60

Value, adding, 2
Villanova University, 126

INDEX

Virtual Try-On, 47–48
Visual cues:
  and development of Wonderopolis, 158
  sparking conversation with, 57, 58
Visual journal of recovery, 77
Voice-to-voice conversations, 169

Walden University, 127
Walmart, 6
Warby Parker (eyewear company), 47–48
Watching TV, chilling and, 6–7
Websites:
  content-driven, 75
  educational, 155
  traffic to, 166
We Love Our Employees Day, 182
Whole Foods Market, 29–31, 187
Wins, short-term, 187–188
Wolfe, David, 102
WOM, *see* Word of mouth
WOMMA, *see* Word of Mouth Marketing
  Association
"Wommology" (presentation), 40
WOMMY awards, 182
Wonder Jar', 158–159
Wonder of the Day', 157–160, 163–164
Wonderopolis, 151, 157–169, 182, 190
  comments from community on, 160
  connecting through, 159–160

creating dialogues with, 163–165
growth of, 161–162
intangibles benefits of, 166
Ed Keller on, 169
Steve Knox on, 168–169
measuring success of, 165
messengers within, 162–163
relationships at, 158, 165–166
visual cues and, 158
and why passion matters, 166–167
and Wonder Jar', 158–159
and Wonder of the Day', 157–160
Wonderopolis Lead Families, 161–162
Word of mouth (WOM):
  for brand-related conversation, 29
  in the classroom, 137
  opportunity with, 41
Word of mouth marketing:
  advocacy as ultimate goal of, 186
  and deciding what gets talked about,
    26–27
  future of, 23–26
  successful strategy for, 89, 141
Word of Mouth Marketing Association
    (WOMMA), 40, 132, 182
Working Out Sucks! (Runyon and Mortensen),
    102, 104

Zappos, 33, 185–186